Introducing the Internet to Young Learners

Ready-to-Go Activities and Lesson Plans

Linda W. Braun

Neal-Schuman Publishers, Inc.

New York   London

Published by Neal-Schuman Publishers, Inc.
100 Varick Street
New York, NY 10013

Copyright © 2001 by Linda W. Braun

The paper used in this publication meets the minimum requirements of
American National Standard for Information Sciences—Permanence for
Paper for Printed Library Materials, ANZI Z39.48–1992.

Printed and bound in the United States of America.

ISBN 1–55570–404–2

Library of Congress Cataloging-in-Publication Data

Braun, Linda W.
    Introducing the Internet to young learners : ready-to-go activities
and lesson plans / Linda W. Braun.
        p. cm.
    Includes bibliographical references and indexes.
    ISBN 1–55570–404–2 (alk. paper)
    1. Internet in education—Handbooks, manuals, etc. 2. Internet—
Study and teaching—Handbooks, manuals, etc. I. Title.

LB1044.87   .B72 2001
372.133'44678—dc 21
                                                            00–051976

Dedication

In memory of Ellen Berne, who was there when this all began.

Table of Contents

List of Figures

List of Activity Sheets

Preface

WHY THIS BOOK

When people ask what I do for a living, they often end up getting a lecture. It never seems possible to simply tell them my job title – educational technology consultant. Instead, I'm compelled to describe one of my missions in life. My goal is to help those who work and live with children figure out techniques for integrating the Internet into educational settings in meaningful ways.

When it comes to asking questions about children and the Internet, all too often people begin by asking the wrong one: "Does the Internet make kids smarter?" Instead, librarians, teachers, and parents need to ask:

- How can we use the Internet to improve student learning?
- What does it take for teachers to integrate the Internet into their classrooms in substantial ways?
- What skills do students need in order to be smart—and safe—Internet users?

All too often we hear about the controversies surrounding children and cyberspace. *Introducing the Internet to Young Learners: Ready-to-Go Activities and Lesson Plans* demonstrates to librarians, teachers, and parents how the Internet is used to enhance children's learning. It also explores ways to answer a powerful question: What true educational opportunities does the Internet offer to children?

WHO IS IT FOR?

This book is intended for librarians, primary school teachers, and parents who want to integrate the Internet into student learning environments. It will help you to:

- Understand the basic functions of the Internet and how these functions work.

- Think creatively about Internet tools and discover innovative uses for the Internet in schools, libraries, and homes.
- Learn why the Internet can be a positive force in education.

WHAT'S INSIDE

Introducing the Internet to Young Learners: Ready-to-Go Activities and Lesson Plans is divided into four units.

The first unit focuses on teaching students how to learn about the Internet. It answers some fundamental questions: What is the Internet? How do I integrate it into the curriculum? What basic skills do students need? Unit 2 concentrates on the World Wide Web – how to explain it to students, teach them about the information available there, and the skills needed to discover it. Exploring e-mail is examined in Unit 3. What is e-mail? What's a mailing list? What can you do with e-mail? In the last unit, we look into chat and instant messaging. After exploring definitions, we find out what students can do with these advanced functions.

Each unit is separated into several sections, including:

Topic Overview

There are, of course, many books that provide in-depth information about how the Internet works. Primary school children do not need this level of technical knowledge of the Internet, or its functions, to provide meaningful learning opportunities. Each unit overview does not provide exhaustive detail about what makes the Internet, the Web, e-mail, or chat work. What the overview does provide is the information a librarian, teacher, or parent needs in order to help children become successful users of the technology. This overview section will help readers with varying levels of knowledge translate the Internet to young students. This section of each unit will prove to be particularly useful to novice Internet users as well as those users who have always felt they would like just a little bit more of an understanding of how the technology works.

School and Library Integration

This section asks librarians, teachers, and parents to think creatively, and perhaps differently, about the use of a particular Internet function in student learning. This is the part of *Introducing the Internet to Young Learners* where you will find examples of how schools and libraries use the technology. I have included ideas and techniques you might use to extend and enhance student Internet use. If you are an educator who feels comfortable with the technical aspects of the Internet and its major components, consider starting with this section of each chapter.

Lesson Plans

The lesson plans in *Introducing the Internet to Young Learners: Ready-to-Go Activities and Lesson Plans* are the core of the book. Designed for easy replication, the lesson plans provide step-by-step examples of how to teach the Internet and the best ways to improve the critical thinking skills of your students. The lessons aim to integrate the Internet into the classroom while building specific Internet skill levels with the children. Suggested extension activities included with each lesson expand the Internet framework into a variety or curriculum areas and topics. The "Curriculum, Internet Skills, and Critical Thinking Matrix," following the preface on page xv gives an overview of what is covered in each lesson.

Reproducible Activity Sheets

A selection of reproducible activity sheets is included at the end of each lesson. These materials are referenced within the lesson plan and correlate with the specific critical thinking and Internet searching skills covered. The activity sheets reinforce the ideas presented within the lesson plan and provide models for ways to help students think critically about, and analyze, the materials they access and use on the Internet. Students can complete many of these sheets as they discover Websites, send e-mail messages, or join in chat sessions. Activity sheets encourage meaningful Internet use as students take time to process and think about the information they locate.

Each chapter also includes a list of print and electronic resources related to the topic and citations for all of the Websites included in the chapter. Website addresses are listed in the "Where Do I Find Out More About..." section. A basic glossary completes each unit.

Appendix A presents Websites that will show you how to help students learn to cite electronic resources. Appendix B provides helpful information literacy resources. Please also note the information on Internet safety in the "Rules for Chat and Instant Messaging Safety" in Unit 4. You'll find URLs of sites with information on Internet safety in the "Find Out More About..." sections of each unit.

HOW TO GET STARTED

Parents and educators need to explore the uses of the Internet and develop learning experiences that harness the technology to enhance student learning. Think of all the Internet resources you use everyday and how they might be turned into learning experiences. (Recently a teacher told me how he uses the eBay auction Website in math lessons for adult basic education classes.) I hope that the ideas, lesson plans, and activities in *Introducing the Internet to Young Learners* will inspire you to be creative in your integration of the Internet in your teaching.

Figure P-1. Curriculum, Internet Skills, and Critical Thinking Matrix

		Playing With Memory	What's in a URL?	Finding Out About Poetry	The Logic of Searches	What's the Difference?	How Good Is It?	What's the Best Price?	What Can You Tell Me About Your State?	What Do You Know About the Middle Ages?	Let's Talk About Space Exploration
Curriculum Connections	Math	*		*	*			*			
	Science	*			*						*
	Language Arts	*	*	*		*	*	*	*	*	*
	History/Social Science					*	*		*	*	*
	Arts	*									
Internet Skills	Navigation	*	*	*		*	*	*	*	*	*
	E-mail								*	*	
	Chat										*
	Searching			*	*			*			
Critical Thinking Skills	Evaluation		*		*	*	*				
	Research			*	*			*	*	*	*
	Information Analysis	*	*	*	*	*	*	*	*	*	*

Acknowledgments

To the librarians and teachers who were students in the training sessions and classes I taught I say thank you. Many of you were willing to explore new ideas and push traditional boundaries in an attempt to figure out the best way to integrate the Internet into learning environments. These sessions helped me formulate some of the strategies, tips, and techniques that are covered in this book.

Thanks to Robert and Lucy for understanding my writing schedule and style.

Carolyn Noah, who is always willing to brainstorm ideas about kids, technology, libraries, and education, also deserves my thanks.

KIDS Report evaluation criteria are reprinted with permission. KIDS Report, *www.kids.library.wisc.edu*, is a project of the University of Wisconsin-Madison Libraries, copyright by the University of Wisconsin System Board of Regents.

ePals logo is reprinted with permission of ePals, *www. epals.com/*

.

Unit 1

Teaching Students How to Learn About the Internet

Can you read the newspaper, listen to the radio, or watch TV without encountering something to do with the Internet? Probably not. The Internet has taken over the conversation of teachers, librarians, parents, and kids around the world. What is it about this medium that has created such a mass interest? Possibly it's the changes that the Internet is bringing to the way students learn, teachers teach, librarians' work, and everyone communicates with each other. This unit covers the basics of what the Internet is, how people access it, and how you can integrate basic Internet skills into the classroom.

WHAT IS THE INTERNET?

You may have heard people say, "The Internet is a network of networks." When hearing that you might have said to yourself, "What does that mean?" Another way to put it is that the Internet is made up of a series of computers all connected to each other and exchanging information from one to another. It's a vast system of computers that are always talking to each other.

What sometimes confuses students, parents, and teachers is the difference between what the Internet is and what are the regularly used functions of the Internet. The Internet is the computers communicating with each other. The functions are what you can do with the Internet.

For example, you can

- Send an e-mail to an expert.
- Surf the Web to find information on a particular topic.
- Chat with an astronaut.

This means that Netscape or Internet Explorer isn't the Internet. The software that a student uses to e-mail a friend isn't the Internet. These are simply tools that enable students, teachers, parents, and librarians to take advantage of specific functions of the Internet.

Not too long ago people would say that in order to connect to the Internet you needed to have a computer with a modem, a phone line, and a provider who sold you service to connect your computer to that network of networks, the Internet. In part this is still true. It's possible to connect to the Internet with a computer, a modem, a phone line, and a provider. But you can also connect using what are called Internet appliances—WebTV, for example.

When using an Internet appliance, students cannot meet all their computing needs—creating and saving files, for example, but these appliances do provide an interface for using the functions of the Internet. Even with an Internet appliance users still need to have a service provider who provides the connection from the appliance to the Internet.

You can connect your computer to the Internet through a low-speed or high-speed (or broadband) connection. A low-speed connection uses a computer modem and a basic phone line. Possible broadband connections include:

- Cable modems (using the same cable lines the local TV or television cable company uses)
- Satellite dishes
- DSL (Digital Subscriber Line that carries data at a high speed over telephone wires)

These high-speed connections are termed broadband because the lines that the information travels through are "broader" than the lines used in a basic telephone modem connection. Of course, the higher the speed of your connection to the Internet, the faster students, parents, and teachers are able to access the resources and functions available.

HOW DO I INTEGRATE THE INTERNET INTO THE CURRICULUM?

You might be asking yourself, "Does every lesson require an Internet component?" The answer is no. Then you might wonder, "When is it appropriate to add the Internet to the curriculum?" That's an important question to which there is no simple answer. You can start, however, by thinking about how (and if) student learning is enhanced through the use of the Internet.

There are several ways that the Internet can enhance or extend student learning. For example:

- Students access materials that would not be available otherwise. The **American Memory** Website sponsored by the Library of Congress provides primary source documents.
- Experts can provide current, accurate, and firsthand information on a topic. **MadSciNet** allows students to ask scientists a question and search the database to locate answers to previously asked questions. Through this Website students get answers from experts and also find information that might not be readily available in their local library, school, or community.
- WebQuests help students focus their research. Students in elementary school have studied the desert for decades using books, magazines, and other print resources to learn about the environment. **The Desert is Ours** Web quest extends students' desert research to include Web resources and aids them in locating information from a wide variety of resources.
- Audio, video, and interactive Website components meet a variety of student learning styles and needs. Students visiting the **Science of Hockey** Website sponsored by the Exploratorium not only read about physics principles inherent in hockey, but they also listen to hockey players talk about the skill required to play the game and view video sequences that demonstrate physics properties. Students who require aural and visual enhancements for their learning are served by a site like this.
- Students submit their art, stories, poems, and so on, for submission to Websites such as **Kids on the Net**. When students know their work is going to be available to people all over the world, they often take more pride in what they create.

In her article, "Integrating Technology: Some Things You Should Know," Laurie B. Dias writes, ". . . technology is integrated when it is used in a seamless manner to support and extend curriculum objectives and to engage students in meaningful learning. It is not something one does separately; it is part of the daily activities taking place in the classroom." (Dias, 1999) Use the above examples and Laurie Dias' statement as your guide as you strive to determine when and how to integrate the Internet effectively and successfully.

WHAT BASIC SKILLS DO STUDENTS NEED?

Much of what can be accomplished with the Internet takes place using the World Wide Web. How the Web works and what you can do with it is discussed in a later unit. However, when students are learning how to use the Web, one thing they need to become familiar with is the Web browser:

- The browser is the software, usually Netscape Navigator or Internet Explorer, on a computer that acts as an interface for accessing the Web.
- The browser allows students to navigate around Websites by clicking on links, typing in addresses, listening to audio, viewing pictures, typing in specific addresses, setting bookmarks, and so forth.
- The basic features of a browser are standard. No matter what browser a student learns to use first the skills are easily transferred to a different piece of browser software.

The aspects of using a browser that students should become familiar with include:

- Knowing the functions of the different toolbars and buttons
- Knowing how to set bookmarks
- Knowing how to type a Web address

Students often know what is accomplished using a Web browser, but they do not always have the skills to do specific tasks at the appropriate time.

It's possible to integrate lessons into the curriculum that teach students basic browser skills while they are at the same time locating information on a particular topic. Internet Web quests and scavenger hunts are popular means of accomplishing this. These lessons present students with questions they need to answer while navigating the Web. Through their search for answers, students are required to maneuver through the Web using the various functions of their browser.

In order to succeed using the Internet, it's essential for students to understand the composition of a Web address. A good way to teach students this is by making a comparison to their home address:

- Ask students what friends and family need to know in order to drive or walk to their house. Part of their answer is that friends and family need to have the street address where their house is.

- Explain that, like a house, each site and page on the Web has an address.
- Tell students that every computer has a specific address and unless they have a way of getting to that address, they can't visit the Website.

You can explain to students that the address is composed of the domain name for the site along with the name of the folder and/or file where the Web pages live. The domain name for a Website tells who owns or sponsors the site and the organization type of the owner/sponsor. Domain names are registered in much the same way as trademarks. The owner of the domain name registers with one of several agencies to own the name.

In the diagram, Figure 1–1, the domain name informs the user that the Website is owned/sponsored by the Exploratorium and that the Exploratorium is registered as an educational institution. When a domain name is registered, the owner of the name registers the name with the suffix—.edu in the example below—that is appropriate to the owning or sponsoring institution. In most instances this suffix is accurate; however, be sure to mention to students there are instances where the suffix does not accurately reflect the type of institution or person that sponsors or owns the Website.

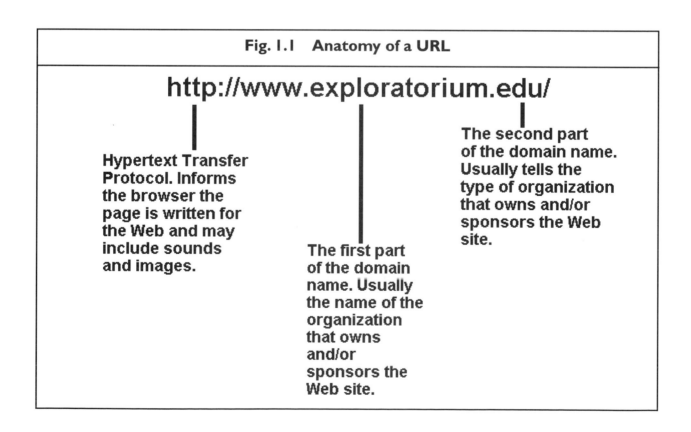

Fig. 1.1 Anatomy of a URL

http://www.exploratorium.edu/

Hypertext Transfer Protocol. Informs the browser the page is written for the Web and may include sounds and images.

The first part of the domain name. Usually the name of the organization that owns and/or sponsors the Web site.

The second part of the domain name. Usually tells the type of organization that owns and/or sponsors the Web site.

Fig. 1.2 Domain Name Suffixes		
Suffix	What it means	Examples
.com	The site is sponsored, or hosted, by a commercial organization.	*www.nike.com/*—**NIKE** *www.aol.com/*—**AOL**
.edu	The site is sponsored, or hosted, by a school— usually a college or university.	*www.harvard.edu/*—**Harvard University** *www.ohio.edu/*—**Ohio University**
.gov	The site is sponsored, or hosted, by a government organization.	*www.fbi.gov/*—**The FBI** *www.nasa.gov/*—**NASA**
.mil	The site is sponsored, or hosted, by the military.	*www.army.mil/*—**The U.S. Army** *www.navy.mil/*—**The U.S. Navy**
.org	The site is sponsored, or hosted, by a non-profit organization.	*www.bostonkids.org/*—**The Children's Museum** *www.4h-usa.org/*—**4H**
.us	The site is sponsored, or hosted, by an organization in the United States. Many schools have addresses.	*http://buckman.pps.k12.or.us/*—**Buckman Elementary School, Portland, Oregon** *www.norfolk.k12.ma.us/*—**Norfolk Public Schools, Norfolk, Massachusetts**
.fr .au .uk, etc.	The site is in a foreign country, for example, France, Australia, or the United Kingdom.	*www.monde-diplomatique.fr/*— **Le Monde diplomatique** *www.csu.edu.au/*—**Charles Stuart University**

In early 2001 seven new suffixes will become available. These include .biz, .info, and .pro. The list above includes what are currently some of the most popular domain name suffixes. As new suffixes are added infrequently, this list is not meant to be inclusive of all that are available.

Fig. 1.3 Adding Bookmarks/Favorites	
Netscape Navigator	**Internet Explorer**
Adding Bookmarks 1. When on the page that you would like to bookmark, select *Bookmarks, Add Bookmark* from the toolbar. **Organizing Bookmarks into Folders** 1. From the toolbar select *Bookmarks, Edit Bookmarks.* 2. A list of your bookmarks is displayed. 3. From the menu bar select *New Folder.* 4. Type in the name of the folder and select *OK.* 5. You will now see the folder you just created on the bookmarks list. 6. It's now possible to drag any of your bookmarks, anything on the list with a bookmark icon, into the folder that you just created. 7. When you have finished creating folders and organizing your bookmarks, select *File, Close* from the menu bar. **Renaming Bookmarks** 1. From the toolbar select *Bookmarks, Edit Bookmarks.* 2. A list of your bookmarks is displayed. 3. Click on the bookmark that you would like to rename in order to highlight it. 4. Select *Edit, Bookmark Properties,* from the menu bar. 5. A box will open with the name and URL of the bookmark you selected. Type in the new name for the bookmark and then select OK. 6. When you have finished renaming bookmarks, select *File, Close* from the menu bar.	**Adding Favorites** 1. When on the page that you would like to add to Favorites, select *Favorites, Add to Favorites,* from the menu bar. 2. A box will open with the name of the site. You can change this name to something else by typing in a new name in the box labeled *Name.* 3. Select *OK.* **Organizing Favorites into Folders** 1. When on the page that you would like to add to Favorites select *Favorites, Add to Favorites* from the menu bar. 2. A box will open with the name of the site. 3. Select the *Create In* button. 4. A window will open with the names of the folders in the Favorites directory of Internet Explorer. 5. If a folder exists in which you would like to place the Favorite, click on the folder to highlight it and select *OK.* 6. If you would like to create a new folder for the Favorite, select *New Folder.* 7. A window will open asking you to type in the name of the new folder. Type the name in the box labeled *Folder Name* and then select *OK.* 8. The window with the list of folders will display with the folder just created highlighted. Select *OK* to place the Favorite in that folder.

HOW CAN TEACHERS AND STUDENTS ORGANIZE WHAT THEY FIND?

Once students start surfing the Web to find information for homework or personal use, they need to learn methods for quickly revisiting favorite and useful sites. Web browser "Bookmarks" (or "Favorites") utilities are a tool students use to organize and manage their access to these sites (see Fig. 1.3). Students may know about bookmarks already. What they might not know is that it's possible to organize bookmarks into folders based on subject, theme, or other organizational structure. For example, imagine students are working on a unit on the Middle Ages. As they perform their research they create a bookmark folder called Middle Ages and place all the bookmarks of Websites they will use in their research in that folder. Then, whenever a student wants to access a Middles Ages site, she clicks on the Middle Ages bookmark folder and selects the site she wants to visit.

In order to use bookmarks to their fullest advantage students need to know that bookmarks can be renamed. Many times a Web page name doesn't clearly define the content of a site or what it is about the site that students find useful. By renaming the bookmark students have a better chance of remembering what information is available at each of the sites on the bookmarks list.

There are a few differences in how bookmarks and favorites are added to the Web browser. However, the overall concept of how these tools can be used remains the same.

Once students learn how to navigate with the Web browser successfully, their Internet experiences will be more productive. The lessons included in this unit provide you with the framework for helping students acquire basic Web navigation skills.

LESSON PLAN—LEARNING BASIC NAVIGATION SKILLS

Overview

In this lesson students look at the "Online Exhibits" section at the Exploratorium **Memory** Website. While doing so they learn how to use basic Web browser features and navigate through a Website. Although this lesson focuses on the memory, you can create a similar lesson using a particular topic or Website that meets your curriculum needs.

Before Getting Started

Visit the **Memory** Website, *www.exploratorium.edu/memory/ index.html*, and become familiar with the different "Online Exhibits" at the site. Make sure that you are familiar with how to navigate through the exhibits before you present the lesson to students. Learn how to go back and forth in an exhibit and how to get back to the **Memory** main page.

The lesson does not include exhibits on the **Memory** site that require the Shockwave plug-in. However, if you have access to that plug-in, you may want to extend this lesson to include those exhibits as well. (To check to see if you have the plug-in select the exhibit titled "Droodles." Select the "Click to Start" link. If the page loads with the images, you have the plug-in. If a window opens telling you you need to download a plug-in, you don't have it yet.)

Lesson Sidebar 1 The Critical Thinking Connection—Navigation

By asking students to think about and articulate orally and in writing how they navigate a Website, you are helping them learn how the Web works. This takes students beyond the simple act of pointing and clicking to thinking about what happens when they point at a link, click the mouse, and go to a new page of content. Students will also start to think about how they make choices about where they go and how they get to the information they need when they visit a Website.

When working on this lesson, give students opportunities to discuss how they navigate a Website and ask questions about how Web navigation works. Be sure to point out that to navigate a site successfully they need to read the information on the page so they can make the good choices about where to go next in their Web browsing and surfing.

Student Prerequisites

- Mouse skills
- Ability to open a program by clicking on the icon

Technology Requirements

- Small group and/or individual computer access
- Internet access
- Access to the World Wide Web
- Shockwave plug-in (optional)

Activity Sheets

- *Common Cents*
- *If You're Going to Rob a Bank Wear a Wig*

Grade Level

- 3 through 5

Curriculum Connections

- Science
- Art
- Language Arts

Internet Skills

- Navigation

Critical Thinking Skills

- Information analysis

Student Outcomes

- Knowledge of Web navigation skills using browser buttons and Website links.
- Ability to articulate orally and in writing Web navigation skills and concepts.
- Ability to read Web page content and make decisions about where to find information at a site.

Extension Activities

- Brainstorm with students memory games to develop for students in another class or group. Divide the class into groups and have each group create one of the memory games on the brainstorming list. When the games are complete, have the other classes or groups try the creations.
- Divide the class into groups. Have each group visit a different Website and write directions for their classmates on how to get around the site. The groups may also want to create questions for their classmates to answer about the content of the site.

Activity Procedure

1. Type in the URL for the Exploratorium **Memory** Website, *www.exploratorium.edu/memory/index.html*, and show students the front page. (As you type in the address point out that you are typing in the address and where on the browser you are typing it.) Mention that students will be working individually or in small groups with the "Common Cents" and "If You're Going to Rob a Bank Wear a Wig" Exhibits.

2. Ask students to tell you how to access the "Common Cents" exhibit and how they know that's the way to do it.

3. Select the "Common Cents" link and ask students how to get back to the main page of the **Memory** Website. See how many different ways you and the students come up with to go back to the main **Memory** page. Ask them to tell you how they go forward to the page they were just on. Again, see how many different ways you and the students come up with to move forward one page. Have students make lists of all the different ways they navigate the Website.

4. Divide students into small groups and distribute the "Common Cents" and the "If You're Going to Rob a Bank Wear a Wig" activity sheets.

5. Give the groups a few minutes to look over the activity sheets to see if they have any questions. When the questions are answered, the students can visit the two exhibits.

6. When the students have finished visiting the exhibits, bring the class together to discuss what they learned in the exhibits. Ask students to explain how they moved around the site and discuss any instances where they had trouble figuring out how to get from one place to another on the site.

Navigation Notes for Teachers

- If in a one-computer classroom, start the lesson by showing students how to access the **Memory** Website. Then have students work in small groups throughout the day in order to finish the activities that make up this lesson. If without a computer projection system, consider printing pages from the site, after getting permission to do so, and discussing site navigation with students as they look at the copied pages.

- At the third-grade level this lesson works very well to teach students how to move around on the Web. It also helps them learn how to look for clues in order to successfully find information on a Web page. At this grade level point out to students that there are often similarities between sections on Websites. For example, many sites have an "about" section, a "feedback" section, and a "search" section. Also, consider drawing a large graphic organizer (for example, a storyboard or flowchart) of the Website for students to fill in as a group. (See Unit 2 for more information on this topic.)

- At the fourth- and fifth-grade levels use the lesson on navigation to help students begin to think about how Websites are organized as a series of pages on a topic. Ask students to create a graphic organizer for the Website (for example, a storyboard or flowchart) that displays how the pages of the site are connected and how the visitor gets from one page to another on the site. (See Unit 2 for more information on this topic.)

- At the fifth-grade level use the lesson on navigating a Website to start a discussion on Website evaluation as it relates to organization of content and design. Ask students to make a list of organization and design criteria they would consider essential to a Website. (See Unit 2 for more information on this topic.)

7. Give the students a chance to try other areas of the exhibit in their small groups.

Website Alternatives

The Websites listed below may be substituted for the **Memory** site to teach navigation skills within another content area.

CREATURES OF THE NIGHT AND YOU (SCIENCE)

http://tqjunior.thinkquest.org/5135/

This is a project created by students for Thinkquest Jr. Its simple navigational structure makes it a good place to begin when thinking about how to move around a Website. Start students by asking them to look at the labels of each of the links on the main page and to try to determine what they think they will find when they click on each link. Then ask students to test their hypothesis by selecting each link. Make sure that as students read and view the information about nocturnal animals they also learn how to open the glossary and then return to the page they were looking at previously.

ODYSSEY ONLINE (HISTORY/SOCIAL SCIENCE)

www.emory.edu/CARLOS/ODYSSEY/index.html

This site is filled with information on ancient civilizations—Greece, Egypt, the Near East, Rome, and Africa. Ask students to focus on the top of the front page, which includes a link for each of the civilizations covered at the site. Then ask students to look at and read the rest of the page and see if they can find the same links anywhere else on the page. When they have found the links at the bottom of the page, ask if they see any similarities between the links at the top of the page and those at the bottom. (They should notice that the images used for each civilization are the same; the format of each is different however.) Students then select a civilization and look at its main page. Ask them to figure out how to locate information about different aspects of the civilization. Students should be sure to notice the links at the bottom of the page. Are they the same as what was available on the main page?

PLIMOTH-ON-WEB (HISTORY/SOCIAL SCIENCE)

www.plimoth.org/

The official site of Plimoth Plantation is a good place to start students in learning basic navigation skills. The site's simple design and layout lends itself to learning how to read a screen to find content and move from page to page reading and collecting information. Start students either with the "Virtual Tour of Plimoth Plantation" or the link labeled "The 1627 Pilgrim Village." If visiting the "Virtual Tour," students should read the screen to figure out how to move forward and back within the tour. Ask them to determine how to look at an enlarged view of an image. If on the "1627 Pilgrim Village" page, ask students to select the links within the main text to find out where they go. Find out where the links on the left side of the page lead. From any section of the site ask students to figure out how to return to the main Plimoth Plantation page.

STARCHILD (SCIENCE)

http://starchild.gsfc.nasa.gov/docs/StarChild/

StarChild provides content on the solar system on two different levels. If teaching third-grade students, focus them on the "Level 1" materials. If teaching fifth-grade students, focus them on the "Level 2" materials. When students first look at the **StarChild** main page, point out the labels under "Level 1" and "Level 2" and ask if they can figure out why the labels are the same under the different headings. Ask students to select the "Solar System" link in the level appropriate to their grade. Have them read the information on the main page of the "Solar System" section and then select one of the links within the main text. What do they find when they select those links? Have the students read the information on the main page of the "Solar System" section and then ask them to select one of the links within the main text of the page at which they are currently looking. After they have read the material on the generated page, ask students to try and get back to the main page of **StarChild** and the "Solar System" introductory page.

WORDCENTRAL (LANGUAGE ARTS)

www.wordcentral.com/

This site gives students a chance to write poems, find out the meaning of different words, create their own dictionary words, and more. At **WordCentral** students point and click on site images to go from one page to another, or they use the drop-down menu available on each page. Using this site you can help students learn how to use both visual images for navigation and special features such as drop-down menus. Older students can draw a graphic organizer of the site using the drop-down menu as their only clue. Then they can check their organizer by clicking through the site to see if they made the right connections. Have younger students start by selecting the image link labeled "Enter the Hallway." Then have them select the image labeled "Cafeteria." Once they are on the page of "Daily Buzzwords," ask students to figure out how to get back to the main page of **WordCentral** and the "Hallway." From the "Hallway" page ask students how to get to the "Second Floor" of the site.

ZOOM (MATH, SCIENCE, HISTORY, LANGUAGE ARTS, ARTS)

www.pbs.org/wgbh/zoom/

The Website for the PBS series of the same name presents opportunities for talking with students about reading the screen in order to figure out where a link leads. On the front page show that, by pointing the mouse over the areas labeled "Zoom Too," "Send It to Zoom," and "Site Map and Search," the labels change to provide more information about what is available in each section. Have students select the "Site Map and Search" image link. Once on that page mention that, by pointing at any of the links listed on the page, the student will see text displayed toward the top of the page explaining what content can be found within that section of the site. When students select one of the internal areas of the site to visit, make sure to ask them to figure out how to get back to the main page of the **Zoom** site and how to get back to the "Site Map and Search" section.

Activity Sheet

Common Cents

Student Name(s):

First Steps
Open the Web browser on your computer.

Type in the address for the Exploratorium **Memory** Website, *www.exploratorium.edu/memory/index.html.*

Select the link for the "Common Cents" Online Exhibit.

Answer These Questions
Which penny did you pick?

Were you correct, and how did you find out if the penny you selected was the correct one?

How many other people selected the same penny that you did? How did you find out how many people picked the same penny?

What did you think of this exhibit? Was it easy or hard for you to pick the right penny? Why do you think it was easy or hard?

After you have answered these questions, go back to the **Memory** main page. How did you get back to the main page? Are there other ways to get back to the main page? What are they?

Activity Sheet

If You're Going to Rob a Bank Wear a Wig

Student Name(s):

First Steps (if you aren't already at the **Memory** Website)
Open the Web browser on your computer.

Type in the address for the Exploratorium **Memory** Website, *www.exploratorium.edu/ memory/index.html.*

Select the link for the "If You're Going to Rob a Bank Wear a Wig" Online Exhibit.

Answer These Questions
Where do you see the name of the exhibit on the Website?

When you select "Continue" where do you end up?

Did you know about the famous people who had Elvis' hair, and how can you find out on the Website who they were?

Can you go back to the main page of the exhibit from the "Elvis Impersonator" page? How do you do that?

Continue through the exhibit until you get to the end. What information is on the last page of the exhibit? How can you be sure this is the last page?

After you have answered these questions go back to the **Memory** main page. How did you get back to the main page? Are there other ways to get back to the main page? What are they?

LESSON PLAN—DISCOVERING THE COMPONENTS OF A URL

Overview

In this lesson students learn how a Web address is constructed and what they can tell about the owner/sponsor of the Website through the URL. They also discuss why it's important to know who is the owner or sponsor of a Website.

Before Getting Started

Make sure that you are familiar with the components of a URL. Spend time surfing the Web to look at URLs and try to determine why the address is constructed as it is. As a way to get the discussion going, ask students to bring in URLs cut out of newspapers or magazines. Alternatively, you could paste URLs from newspapers and magazines around the classroom and start the discussion by having students look at those.

Student Prerequisites

- Preliminary exposure to URLs
- Beginning Web navigation skills

Technology Requirements

- Small group or individual computer access
- Internet access
- Access to the World Wide Web

Lesson Sidebar 2 The Critical Thinking Connection—Web Addresses

It might seem obvious to you that the ownership of a Website says something important about the authority and accuracy of the information presented. That connection will not be as obvious to students. As you work with students to teach them about the construction of a Web address, be sure to point out why the domain name suffix is important. Seek out examples that demonstrate how information can be presented differently depending on who presents that information. Provide opportunities for students to compare information on the same topic in different formats (books, magazines, radio, television, and the Web) and from different points of view.

Activity Sheets

- What's in a URL?
- What's the Suffix?
- Tell Me About These URLs

Grade Level

- 3 through 5

Curriculum Connections

- Language Arts

Internet Skills

- Navigation

Critical Thinking Skills

- Evaluation
- Information analysis

Student Outcomes

- Ability to look at a Web address and determine the owner or sponsor from the domain name.
- Ability to articulate orally and in writing how a Website address is constructed.

Extension Activities

- Now that the students know how URLs are constructed, see if they can figure out the Website address for the companys that create their favorite products. (Many company Websites are constructed with the "name of company.com" configuration. For example, the **Disney** Website is *www.disney.com/*.) Ask students to bring in something from home for which they would like to find a Website. See if the students can find the company name on the product. Then ask them to predict Website address for that company. Let them try their predictions on the Web. (Whenever possible check out the URLs before the students. There are instances where an expected address takes students to a site that may not be appropriate.)

• Take a field trip with students to an organization or institution that you visit on the Web. Compare the Web address with the mailing address and have students dissect the different pieces of each. Students can write directions for getting from the school to the live location and instructions on how to get to the Web location.

Activity Procedure

1. Distribute the *What's In a URL?* and *What's the Suffix?* activity sheets. Discuss with the students the different parts of a URL and what they mean. Make sure to point out to students that there are times when the suffix isn't accurate. However, in most instances it is possible to tell what kind of organization sponsors or owns the Website through the suffix. Have students make comparisons between a house or business address and the address of a Website.
2. Divide the students into small groups. Distribute the activity sheet *Tell Me About These URLs*. Ask students to predict the owner/sponsor of each Website listed on the sheet.
3. Brainstorm with students ways they can find out if their predictions are correct. Generate a list of methods they will use. Make sure to include on the list methods for locating information on a Website about the owner/sponsor. This should include looking for a link that has the label "About This Website," or a similar label.
4. Once the class has developed a list of methods for finding out if their predictions are correct, have each team visit one of the Websites to check the accuracy of their answers.
5. Bring the class back together to talk about determining ownership/sponsorship of a Website through the URL. Discuss how easy, or difficult, it was for the students and how accurate they were at determining the owner/sponsor by just looking at the address. Make sure to point out that this is not an exact science and sometimes the URL of the site isn't a completely foolproof way of determining ownership/sponsorship. Discuss again with the class why it's important to be able to tell who is the owner or sponsor of a site.

Website Alternatives

The Websites listed on the following pages may be substituted for those listed on the *Tell Me About These URLs* activity sheet.

Web Address Notes for Teachers

- If in a one-computer classroom, after introducing the lesson, have students complete the worksheet in their small groups. Then throughout the day allow small groups of students to visit the Websites in order to finish the activity. After all of the groups have completed the activity, bring the class back together to talk about the experience. If you have a projection system available you can work as a whole class to check on the ownership and sponsorship of each of the Websites.
- At the third-grade level it may be easier for students to focus on businesses, schools, and organizations with which they are already familiar, for example, the local (or nearby) school system, newspaper, college, or museum.
- At the fifth-grade level expand the lesson to include how domain names are registered and make the comparison between registering for a domain name and a trademark. Include a visit to the **United States Patent and Trademarks** Web page, *www.uspto.gov/web/offices/ac/ahrpa/opa/kids/kidprimer.html*, that explains to students what patents and trademarks are.

.COM SITES

CRAYOLA (ART)

www.crayola.com/

Everything you wanted to know about crayons is at this site.

EXPEDITIONS@NATIONAL GEOGRAPHIC.COM (HISTORY/SOCIAL SCIENCE)

www.nationalgeographic.com/xpeditions/main.html

An atlas of the world is just one of the tools available at this site.

HOW STUFF WORKS (SCIENCE)

www.howstuffworks.com/

Find out how everything from a submarine to DSL works.

PILKEY'S WEBSITE OF FUN (LANGUAGE ARTS)

www.pilkey.com/

This is the Website of children's book author/illustrator Dav Pilkey.

PLANE MATH (MATH)

www.planemath.com/

All of these math activities have something to do with aeronautics.

YOUNG COMPOSERS (MUSIC)

www.youngcomposers.com/

Music written and performed by children is available at this site.

.EDU SITES

THE ART ROOM (ART)

www.arts.ufl.edu/art/rt_room/index.html

Students learn about art and create some of their own.

ASK DR. MATH (MATH)

http://forum.swarthmore.edu/dr.math/index.html

Students get answers to their math questions.

ASK DR. UNIVERSE (LANGUAGE ARTS, HISTORY/SOCIAL SCIENCE, MATH, SCIENCE)

www.wsu.edu/DrUniverse/Contents.html

Science questions and answers can be found here.

BIOGRAPHY MAKER (HISTORY/SOCIAL SCIENCE)

www.bham.wednet.edu/bio/biomaker.htm

This site is all about the art of writing biographies.

JUICE BOTTLE JINGLES (MUSIC, SCIENCE)

www.lhs.berkeley.edu/shockwave/jar.html

Students play songs on juice bottles and learn about the properties of sound.

Treasures@Sea (Science, Language Arts)

www.fi.edu/fellows/fellow8/dec98/

Learn about the ocean through literature.

.GOV SITES

American Memory (History/Social Science)

http://memory.loc.gov/

Primary source documents of all kinds are supplied by the Library of Congress.

Mega-Mathematics (Math)

www.c3.lanl.gov/mega-math/

The math activities and games here cover a wide array of concepts.

NOAA Photo Collection (Science)

www.photolib.noaa.gov/

This is a collection of public domain photos from the National Oceanic and Atmospheric Administration.

.ORG SITES

Art Safari (Art, Language Arts)

http://artsafari.moma.org/

Students write stories to go along with well-known pieces of art.

Bookhive (Language Arts)

www.bookhive.org/

Search for book reviews on a wide array of topics.

Journey North (Science)

www.learner.org/jnorth/

Journey North invites students to track animal and plant migrations.

MIDDLE AGES (HISTORY/SOCIAL SCIENCE)

www.learner.org/exhibits/middleages/

What was it really like to live during the Middle Ages?

MIGHTY M&M MATH PROJECT (MATH)

http://mighty-mm-math.caffeinated.org/main.htm

Compare the percentage of m&m colors in your bag with those from a school somewhere else in the country.

SOUND IS ENERGY (MUSIC, SCIENCE)

http://tqjunior.thinkquest.org/5116/sound.htm

This Thinkquest Jr. winner was created by students to teach about the instruments in the orchestra.

.US SITES

FROM WINDMILLS TO WHIRLIGIGS (ART, SCIENCE)

www.smm.org/sln/vollis/

The art of the whirligig and the scientific principles that make them work are at this site.

A GUIDE TO MEDIEVAL AND RENAISSANCE INSTRUMENTS (MUSIC, HISTORY/SOCIAL SCIENCE)

www.s-hamilton.k12.ia.us/antiqua/instrumt.html

Images and text teach about instruments from these historic time periods.

PLANET EARTH (SCIENCE)

http://powayusd.sdcoe.k12.ca.us/mtr/PlanetEarthMainPage.htm

Online ecology activities for students are at Planet Earth.

STORYBOOK LIBRARY (LANGUAGE ARTS)

www2.northstar.k12.ak.us/schools/upk/books/books.html

The stories here were written for kids by kids.

TURN-OF-THE-CENTURY CHILD (HISTORY/SOCIAL SCIENCE)

www.nueva.pvt.k12.ca.us/~debbie/library/cur/20c/turn.html

What was it like to grow up at the turn of the century?

Activity Sheet

What's in a URL?

Student Name:

http://www.exploratorium.edu/

Hypertext Transfer Protocol. Informs the browser the page is written for the Web and may include sounds and images.

The first part of the domain name. Usually the name of the organization that owns and/or sponsors the Web site.

The second part of the domain name. Usually tells the type of organization that owns and/or sponsors the Web site.

Activity Sheet

What's the Suffix

Student Name:

Use this chart to find out what different domain names mean.

Fig. 1.2 Domain Name Suffixes

Suffix	What it means	Examples
.com	The site is sponsored, or hosted, by a commercial organization.	*www.nike.com/*—**NIKE** *www.aol.com/*—**AOL**
.edu	The site is sponsored, or hosted, by a school— usually a college or university.	*www.harvard.edu/*—**Harvard University** *www.ohio.edu/*—**Ohio University**
.gov	The site is sponsored, or hosted, by a government organization.	*www.fbi.gov/*—**The FBI** *www.nasa.gov/*—**NASA**
.mil	The site is sponsored, or hosted, by the military.	*www.army.mil/*—**The U.S. Army** *www.navy.mil/*—**The U.S. Navy**
.org	The site is sponsored, or hosted, by a non-profit organization.	*www.bostonkids.org/*—**The Children's Museum** *www.4h-usa.org/*—**4H**
.us	The site is sponsored, or hosted, by an organization in the United States. Many schools have .us addresses.	*http://buckman.pps.k12.or.us/*—**Buckman Elementary School, Portland, Oregon** *www.norfolk.k12.ma.us/*—**Norfolk Public Schools, Norfolk, Massachusetts**
.fr .au .uk, etc.	The site is in a foreign country, for example, France, Australia, or the United Kingdom.	*www.monde-diplomatique.fr/*—**Le Monde diplomatique** *www.csu.edu.au/*—**Charles Stuart University**

Activity Sheet

Tell Me About These URLs

Student Name(s):

For each of the Web addresses on the left, record on the right what you think the name of the owner/sponsor of the site is, the type of organization that owns or sponsors the site, how you came up with those answers, and what you can tell about the site by having that information.

URL	Owner/Sponsor—How do you know?	What does knowing who the owner/sponsor is tell you about the site?
www.nytimes.com/		
www.ucla.edu/		
www.usps.gov/		
www.pbs.org/wgbh/lions/		
www.phila.k12.pa.us/ schools/annefrank/		

WHERE DO I FIND OUT MORE ABOUT INTERNET BASICS?

This is a list of resources mentioned in this unit, along with other materials on basic Internet skills and how you can integrate them into the classroom.

Adobe Acrobat Reader

www.adobe.com/products/acrobat/readermain.html

Visit the Adobe site to download the Reader plug-in so you can access .pdf files with your browser.

American Memory

http://memory.loc.gov/

From the Library of Congress, here is a searchable database of primary source documents from America's past and present.

Apple Quicktime

www.apple.com/quicktime/

At the Apple site you can download Quicktime in order to access audio and video content on the Web.

The Desert is Ours

http://coe.west.asu.edu/students/stennille/ST3/desertwq.htm

Students learn about the desert in order to build a miniature botanical garden.

Exploratorium

www.exploratorium.edu/

This is the Website for the Exploratorium museum in San Francisco.

Exploratorium Memory Website

www.exploratorium.edu/memory/index.html

This Exploratorium sub-site includes activities and information about memory.

Internet Explorer

www.microsoft.com/windows/ie/

Go here to download the latest version of Internet Explorer.

Internet 101

www2.famvid.com/i101/

Begin with the links labeled "The Internet" and "Getting Started" to learn Internet basics.

Kids on the Net

http://trace.ntu.ac.uk/kotn/gokids.htm

Students publish their writing and read what others have written.

Macromedia Shockwave

www.macromedia.com/downloads/

Shockwave is a plug-in needed in order to access some forms of interactive Web content.

MadSciNet

www.madsci.org/

Can't find the answer to a science question? Maybe a mad scientist can help.

Netscape Navigator

http://home.netscape.com/

This is where you'll find the latest version of Netscape Navigator to download.

Net EZ User—Connecting

www.zdnet.com/yil/content/netezuser/connecting/index.html

Brought to you by Yahoo! Internet Life, these pages detail the different types of connections available.

NetLingo.com

www.netlingo.com/

Don't know what an Internet term means? Look it up at NetLingo.com.

No More World Wide Wait: Fast Net Access Is Here

www.cnet.com/category/topic/0,10000,0–3762–7–277352,00.html?tag=st.cn.sr.inet.1

This article at C|Net clearly explains the various options available for high-speed Internet connections.

RealPlayer

www.realplayer.com/

At the RealPlayer site you can download the plug-in required to access some audio and video content on the Web.

Science of Hockey

www.exploratorium.edu/hockey/index.html

Students learn how principles of physics play a role in hockey.

The WebQuest Page

http://edweb.sdsu.edu/webquest/webquest.html

Learn what a Web quest is, how to create one, and what others have done with the format.

BASIC INTERNET GLOSSARY

Back

The button on a Web browser that allows you to go back (one page) to the page you were looking at previously.

Bookmarks (see also Favorites)

The utility in Netscape Navigator that allows users to save the address of a Website in order to easily retrieve it over and over again.

Browser

The software that enables users to access the World Wide Web, including still and moving images and sounds.

Cable Modem

The type of modem used to connect to the Internet via lines usually provided by the local TV cable company.

Chat

Talking with other people over the Internet in "real time."

Domain Name

The name of the Website on which a computer lives. Domain names are registered to and owned by a person or organization.

Download

Transferring files from another computer to your own computer.

DSL (Digital Subscriber Line)

Connecting at a high speed to the Internet via copper telephone wires.

E-mail

Communicating with others by sending a message over the Internet.

Favorites

The utility in Internet Explorer for saving Website addresses that will be visited over and over again.

Forward

The browser feature used for moving ahead (one page) to a page that was accessed previously.

History

Websites recently visited that are stored in the browser's memory.

Home

The Web page that is designated in the user's browser as the page to access every time the browser is opened or when the "home" button is selected.

Home Page

The main page of a Website.

HTML (Hypertext Markup Language)

A programming language used to create basic Web pages.

HTTP (Hypertext Transfer Protocol)

How computers talk to each other on the Web.

Hyperlink

A word, sound, or image on a Web page that, when selected, leads to another word or image on the same or a different page.

Instant Messaging (IM)

Sending messages in "real" time to others who are on the Internet at the same time.

Internet

Computers that are connected to each other that allow users to send e-mail, surf the Web, chat, transfer files, and so forth.

Internet Explorer (see also Browser)

A piece of software that allows users to access the features of the Web.

Java

A programming language for creating interactive components for Websites.

Javascript

A programming language for creating interactive components for Websites.

Links (see Hyperlink)

Netscape Navigator (see also Browser)

A piece of software that allows users to access the features of the Web.

.pdf (Portable Document Format)

A way in which files are compressed and saved and made available for display within a Web browser. To view .pdf files the Adobe Acro–bat .pdf Reader plug-in must be installed on the computer.

Plug-In

A computer program that allows Web browsers to access different forms of content—animation, movies, files, and so on. Common plug-ins are Shockwave, Quicktime, Adobe Acrobat Reader, and RealPlayer. Plug-ins have to be downloaded and installed on a computer.

Reload

A Netscape Navigator feature that, when selected, tells the browser to go out on the Internet and retrieve the current page again.

Refresh

An Internet Explorer feature that, when selected, tells the browser to go out on the Internet and retrieve the current page again.

Search Directory

A database of Websites usually organized into subject categories.

Search Engine

An index of Websites that is searchable by keywords and phrases.

Stop

A feature of Netscape Navigator and Internet Explorer. When the "Stop" button is selected on the browser, the page that is currently loading will cease to load.

URL (Uniform Resource Locator)

The address of a Website.

Web Page

A single page on a topic, usually part of a larger Website.

Website

A collection of pages on a particular topic.

World Wide Web

The collection of sites on the Internet connected via hyperlinks. Commonly referred to as "the Web."

Note

1. Dias, Laurie B. (1999) "Integrating Technology: Some Things You Should Know." *Learning and Leading with Technology* (November): 10–13.

Unit 2

Discovering the World Wide Web

When students think of the Internet, they often think of the World Wide Web. Among other things, the Web is the place they can go to locate information for a project, buy books and music, and play games. Before the Web, the Internet was a place filled only with text—no sounds or images were in sight. Without images and sounds the Internet wasn't a student-friendly environment. In this unit you'll find out what you can do to integrate the Web into your classroom and learn what makes the Web work.

WHAT IS THE WORLD WIDE WEB?

Close your eyes and imagine what a spider Web looks like. Do you see lots of thin, delicate threads connecting to each other in a maze-like pattern that provides the backbone of the spider's home? That's not so different than what the World Wide Web looks like. On the Web a page connects to another page. That page connects to another page. Sometimes all the connected pages lead back to where they started. Sometimes they don't. However, all the pages that are connected are usually all linked by a common idea (or thread).

You can show students how this works by creating a graphic representation of a specific Website. Fig 2.1 shows an example from the front page of the **America's Story at America's Library** Website.

What makes the World Wide Web so popular is that it transformed the Internet from a world of text, which required burrowing and digging in order to access materials, to an environment filled with text,

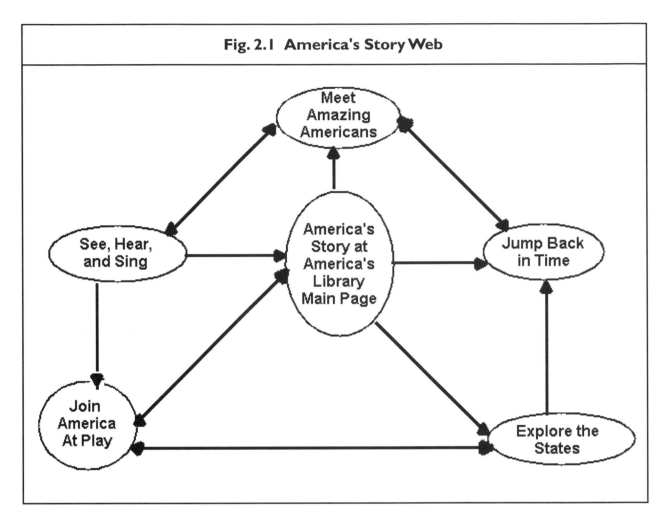

Fig. 2.1 America's Story Web

sound, and images where one mouse click leads a student to just what she is looking for. What makes the World Wide Web so confusing is that almost anyone can publish materials for the Web. The result is that lots of people and organizations have created Web pages and/or sites. There are millions and millions of Web pages created by everyone from a scientist at M.I.T. to one of the students in your class.

Web pages are put together using a specific code. This code tells the Web browser how to display the information on the page. It informs the browser if there are images to display on the page, the size the images should be, the size and color of the text on the page, and so on. Students can look at the code for a page by selecting the "View" item from the top menu bar of the browser and then selecting "Source" from the menu that displays. Looking at the source code helps students begin to understand that Web pages, and sites, are created by people who make decisions about the content of a page, about how a page should be laid out, and about the page's overall colors and design.

As students start to consider how a Web page is put together, it's also important that they think about the difference between a Website and a Web page. Most likely if you ask students to close their eyes and picture a book, they will see in their heads a whole book and not just one of the pages within the book. However, that's not how it usually works with the Web. If you asked students to close their eyes and picture a Website, often what they will see in their heads is one page from within the site and not an image of the entire site. In fact, often students might not even realize that the page they are looking at is a part of a larger Website.

It's not appropriate to evaluate a book based solely on the content of one page, and it's not appropriate to evaluate a Website based solely on the content of one page. If students take one page out of a book, the information on that page may make sense, but most likely it will be out of context and not have the same authority and impact as when it's considered within the whole of the book. When you evaluate the full contents of a book, you can put everything into its proper context and evaluate the authority and validity of the content based on that whole.

The same is true of the Web. Usually, there are a set of pages that make up a Website and that provide a complete picture of what's available on the topic of the site. It's important to not just consider the contents of one page of the site, but to look at the whole set of pages to determine if it is appropriate to the needs of students.

How do you tell if students are looking at a page within a site? There's a couple of ways to figure it out:

- First, if there is a link to "Home," "Main Page," or something similar, you can be pretty certain that students are on a page within a site.
- Sometimes it's as easy as reading the text on the page. Does it say that the page is the main page for a site? If so, then that must mean students are at the front door of a Website.

Also, have students look at the URL. For example:

- The URL for a page within the **America's Story at America's Library** site at the Library of Congress is *www.americaslibrary.gov/about/welcome.html*.
- If you take away the *about/welcome.html* in order to leave the domain name, you'll be at the main page of the site.

If someone has a site mounted on a public server, for example AOL or Geocities, you don't want students to go back as far as the domain name to find the main page. Instead, have them go back in the URL piece by piece until they find the main page for the site. For example:

- If the site was at **About.com** with the address of *http:// kidsbooks.about.com/kids/kidsbooks/library/bl060100.htm*, students would first go back to *kidsbooks.about.com/kids/kidsbooks/ library/*.
- Then if that weren't the main page, they would go to *kidsbooks.about.com/kids/kidsbooks/*.
- Continue to backtrack on the URL until students find the first page of the site. (As students backtrack they should make sure to read portions of the content on each page they uncover. That way they'll be able to tell through both the URL and the text on the page when they have made it to the front door of the site.)

WHAT CAN I DO WITH THE WORLD WIDE WEB?

The answer to the question "What can I do with the Internet?" is a lot. Although teachers, librarians, and parents often think of the Web as primarily a research tool, there are other ways to use the Web as well, some of these are:

- Telecollaborative projects where students exchange data with other students and professionals from around the world.
- Interactive Websites where students learn about a particular topic by taking part in the interactivity.
- E-commerce sites where students gather information about prices for different items and use those to develop math skills.

Once the students are comfortable with navigating the Web, you'll find that they are ready to take part in some of the learning opportunities available. For example, if students are studying the expedition of Lewis and Clark, they can visit the **National Geographic** site where visitors travel the trail with the explorers, making decisions along the way about what happens during the journey.

If students learn about patterns, set theory, graphing, or other related math topics, taking part in the **Mighty m&m Math Project** would enhance learning. For the project students collect data about the contents of bags of m&ms. They then submit their data to the Website and compare their own findings with findings of classrooms from around the country. There are also interesting ways that e-commerce comparison sites can be used to teach math. Try having students use these tools to search for the cost of a particular product across several e-commerce sites. They then can calculate differences among the prices collected.

The point is, that although the Web is a place to research class-

Fig. 2.2 Evaluation Criteria from KIDS Report

Design Features
- Is organized and easy to find your way around
- Contains an explanation of what the page is about
- Contains a reasonable amount of information
- Presents tables, graphics, etc., that are readable
- Is visually interesting with pictures, color, sound and/or video

Ease of Use
- Loads in a reasonable amount to time and is consistently available
- Works easily to go to other links and return to the main page
- Has links to other sites that work
- Identifies helper applications clearly

Content
- Has a title that tells what the site is about
- Presents meaningful and useful content that is intended to educate, inform, or entertain
- Presents information that is easy to read
- Includes content that has correct spelling and grammar
- Includes content that is current when appropriate for the topic
- Provides links to additional information
- Includes pictures that contribute to the overall appearance or are relevant to the content

Credibility
- Includes the author's name and e-mail address and/or information about the author
- Includes a date when the page was last updated
- Includes resources used to develop the information
- Does not request fees or names to use the site

room topics, it's also an environment rich with materials for integrating into lesson plans on a wide variety of topics and in order to learn a diverse number of skills.

Teaching How to Evaluate Information

The Web presents a perfect opportunity for teaching students how to evaluate information. Students need to learn about differences between the information presented in Web form and in book or magazine form. They need to learn that the information presented by an eight-year-old is different than that presented by a college professor. The **KIDS Report** Website provides a model for teaching students evaluation skills. **KIDS Report** gives students a chance to evaluate Websites and post their findings on the Web. The set of criteria is shown in Fig 2.2.

Teaching How to Search for Information

Along with evaluation, it's also important for students to understand how to locate information published on the Web. The difficulty is that there are many different finding tools and no two tools work exactly the same way.

One way to teach students about the differences between search tools is to compare them to the library catalog. Any student who has used a library catalog might know that the catalog contains information on resources that are a part of the library's collection. Remind students that the catalog usually includes information on the author, title, and subject of a book. So, if a student is looking for a book by a particular author, it is possible to look it up in the catalog. If a student is looking for a book with a particular title, it is possible to look it up in the catalog. If a student is looking for a book on a particular subject, it is possible to look it up in the catalog.

What students can't do is look for every instance that a particular word or phrase is used in the books in the library. If that were possible, the catalog would probably be larger than the library itself, and every book on the library's shelves would have to be indexed word for word.

How the different Internet search tools work is very similar to what students accomplish when using a library catalog. For example, search directories—such as **Yahoo!**—search only for items that are included in their database of sites. People (sometimes referred to as editors) maintain these directories by adding sites to the database on a regular basis. They index the sites by subject. Sites that students access when doing a search in an Internet directory are only those that have been added to the database by the editors.

There are small search directories that index either sites on a specific topic—for example, sites on physics—or sites that are reviewed, evaluated, and annotated by the staff of the particular tool—**Librarians' Index to the Internet,** for example. These tools can be extremely useful for students to use for two reasons. First, these tools are smaller in scope so students are not required to filter through as much information in order to find what they are looking for. Second, the sites in the database are evaluated prior to being added. If the evaluators at the tool are people you believe know how to select sites that are good for student use, then you should feel comfortable that the resources in the directory will be acceptable for the students in your class.

If a library catalog indexed every word in every book in the library, it would be similar to a search engine such as HotBot. Search engines use software programs to explore the Internet to find Web pages to add to the index. Humans don't look at the sites before they are added. Instead, the software is programmed to look for certain kinds of information. Many of these search engines index words on Web pages. That makes it possible for you to type in a word and find all the pages where that word appears.

When using any search tool, students need to develop the best search strategy possible. That means they need to figure out how the search tool works and what words or phrases will work best in that tool. One of the best ways to do this is to have students read the "Help" information at the search tool before using it in a search.

If students search a directory like **Yahoo!** or **KidsClick!**, it is important for them to remember that not every word on every Web page is indexed there. Instead, in order to locate the information they are looking for, they have to use the specific words or phrases each tool uses in its indexing. For example, students might be looking for information on a children's book author. They type in the author's name in one of the directories but don't find anything. That's because there isn't a site title, description, or subject heading in the database that includes the author's name. However, if the students' search for the phrase "children's authors," it's very likely they will find a resource that includes information on the author they are studying.

Search tools change and grow on a regular basis, so it's important to read each site's "Help" section prior to using it.

The Web provides a wealth of opportunities for gathering and analyzing information and for learning a wide variety of skills. The lesson plans included in this unit provide a framework for accomplishing some of that gathering, analyzing, and skill building.

LESSON PLAN—MAKING COMPARISONS BETWEEN BOOKS AND WEBSITES

Overview

When teaching students about the Web, it can be useful to make comparisons to a book. In this lesson students brainstorm the different parts of a book and the different parts of a Website.

Before Getting Started

Visit the **Internet Public Library Presidents of the United States** Website, *www.ipl.org/ref/POTUS/*, before beginning the lesson with students. Look at the site to determine what comparisons can be made between a book about the presidents and the Website. Visit the library and check out books on the presidents that the students can use as they make their own comparison.

Some comparisons that can be made include:

Book	Web
Cover	Main page/home page
Table of contents	Links
Index	Search tool
Publisher	Website owner, sponsor, or host
Author	Author
Copyright	Copyright
Images	Images

Lesson Sidebar 3 The Critical Thinking Connection—Books vs. the Web

Helping students to understand the similarities and differences between resources is an effective means of ensuring they are able to make good choices about what research tool to use and when to use it. As you talk about the similarities and differences with students, also discuss the pros and cons of using the different tools and give suggestions about when and why to use each. This lesson is also a good choice for reminding students about Website evaluation criteria. Take time to discuss how students evaluate books and how that process can be replicated for Websites.

Student Prerequisites

- Beginning knowledge of Web navigation
- Familiarity with the basic components of a Website

Technology Requirements

- Small group and/or individual computer access
- Internet access
- Access to the World Wide Web

Activity Sheets

- *What's the Difference?*

Grade Level

- Grades 3 through 5

Curriculum Connections

- Language Arts
- History/Social Science

Internet Skills

- Navigation

Critical Thinking Skills

- Evaluation
- Information analysis

Student Outcomes

- Knowledge of the different components of a Website.
- Ability to articulate orally and in writing the differences and similarities between a book and a Website.

Extension Activity

- Have students compare the number of pages in a book on the presidents with the number of pages at the **Internet Public**

Library Presidents of the United States Website. Ask them to brainstorm the different methods they could use to find all the pages on the Website. Once they have collected the data, ask them to create a graph showing the number of pages of each.

Activity Procedure

1. Tell students they are going to uncover the differences and similarities between books and Websites. Explain they will be doing this by comparing a book and a Website about presidents.
2. Distribute the activity sheet *What's the Difference?* Distribute books on the presidents to students and then have the whole class brainstorm the different components of a book. Ask students to record the different components on the activity sheet.
3. Show students the **Internet Public Library Presidents of the United States** Website. Go through the site and have students see if they can find Website components that match those they recorded for books.
4. If students come up with components that are different from a book, have them add those at the bottom of the *What's the Difference?* activity sheet.
5. After students have come up with a full list of similarities and differences, divide them into groups and ask them to write definitions for each of the Website components which you will publish as a class book and Website dictionary.

Books vs. Websites Notes for Teachers

- This lesson can be very successful in a one-computer classroom as the entire lesson can be completed in a full class with the use of a computer projection system. If a computer projection system is not available, consider copying pages from a Website, after obtaining permission, and ask students to make the comparisons based on the photocopied pages.
- At the third-grade level this lesson provides students with the chance to learn about the parts of a book at the same time they are learning about the parts of a Website. With third-graders focus the comparison on the basic features of each informational source (for example, table of contents and links, cover and main page, copyright, and so on).
- At the fourth- and fifth-grade levels extend this lesson to include evaluation of books and Websites. As students compare the two types of resources, they can also develop criteria for evaluation of the materials.
- At the fifth-grade level extend the comparison to specific types of resources (for example, have students compare a book of fiction with a Website devoted to fiction writing, a book about American history with a Website about American history, and so on).

Website Alternatives

The Websites listed below may be substituted for the **Internet Public Library Presidents of the United States** Website. As students explore each of these Websites:

- Make sure they look for information related to the author, copyright, and owner/sponsor of the Website.
- They should compare the skills required to find author, copyright, and owner/sponsor information at a Website with locating the same information in a book.
- Consider the implications of no author listing on certain sites. Ask students to see if they can find a book that doesn't include an author's (or editor's) name. Ask them to consider when it is appropriate (or if it is ever appropriate) to not know the name and/or credentials of the author of a book or Website.

ALL ABOUT LOBSTERS (SCIENCE)

http://octopus.gma.org/lobsters/

Students learn about the lobster life cycle and lobstering at this Website.

AVMA ALL ABOUT PETS (SCIENCE)

www.avma.org/care4pets/

The American Veterinary Medical Association created this site filled with information about acquiring and keeping pets. The front page of the site is a good example of a Web table of contents.

THE BATTLE OF SARATOGA (HISTORY/SOCIAL SCIENCE)

www.saratoga.org/battle1777/

The Website tells all about the Battle of Saratoga and includes information from both the British and the American perspective.

THE BUBBLESPHERE (SCIENCE)

www.bubbles.org/

The title says it all—this site has everything one might want to know about bubbles. As students compare this site to books on the same topic, be sure they consider the search tool that is available. Ask students to think about the difference or similarity between the index of a book and the search tool.

EXPLORE AND LEARN: THE METROPOLITAN MUSEUM OF ART (ART, HISTORY/SOCIAL SCIENCE)

www.metmuseum.org/explore/index.asp

At this Website students learn about different artists and art styles. Showing students the search tool on this site gives you a chance to compare Website searching with the index of a book. Ask students to see if they can compare the "Site Index" to any particular section of a book.

GIGGLE POETRY (LANGUAGE ARTS)

www.gigglepoetry.com/index.cfm

This is a Website where students can read poetry and write their own. As students explore **Giggle Poetry**, ask them to think about the interactivity of the site (being able to submit poems) versus the static nature of a book.

WELCOME TO THE 1960s (HISTORY/SOCIAL SCIENCE)

www2.lhric.org/pocantico/century/1960s.htm

This site was created by eighth grade students and provides information on the cultural and political highlights of each year in the decade. As students compare this site to a book, make sure that they look at the "Reference" list and consider where that type of information is found in a print volume. Ask them to also try to find out how many different authors there are for the site and see if they can find any books that have multiple authors.

THE WORLD OF MEASUREMENT (MATH)

www.richmond.edu/~ed344/Webunits/measurement/home.htm

At this site students will find information about different forms of measurement, including length, mass, temperature, and time. As students compare this site to book resources, make sure to point out the "Credits and Reproduction" section of the site. Ask students to determine what part of a book equates to this section. Also, this site includes information about awards the site has won. Ask students if books ever have the same kind of information available.

Lesson Activity Sheet

What's the Difference?

Student Name(s):

In the table below record the components of a book on the left and then record the matching components of a Website on the right.

Book Way	Web Way

LESSON PLAN—COMING UP WITH SEARCH TERMS

Overview

One of the most frustrating aspects of searching is coming up with the right terms to use in a search. This lesson uses brainstorming for figuring out possible terms and asks students to use different search tools to compare results when using different search terms. This lesson uses poetry as a jumping off point. You can, of course, use a topic appropriate to your curriculum.

Before Getting Started

Try searching for poetry information at each of the search tools included in this lesson (**KidsClick!**, *www.kidsclick.org/*, and **Yahooligans!**, *www.yahooligans.com/*) before asking students to try the search. Read the "Help" information at each tool to learn more about how it works. Consider the types of problems that students will encounter when trying the search and know how they should handle each of them.

Student Prerequisites

- Beginning knowledge of poets and poetry
- Web navigation skills

Technology Requirements

- Individual or small group computer access
- Internet access
- Access to the World Wide Web

Lesson Sidebar 4 The Critical Thinking Connection—Searching

Often Internet searchers prefer to pursue a search without taking time to plan their search strategy. One of the most important Internet skills you can teach students is the search planning process. While students are working on this lesson, remind them of the need to consider how to present their search topic to a search tool in order to retrieve the best results possible. Also, remind them of the importance of analyzing a search results list in order to find those resources that will best meet their research needs.

Activity Sheets

- *Poetry Questions and Words*
- *Words and What They Lead To*
- *Go with the Flow*
- *Working with the Results*

Grade Level

- Grades 4 and 5

Curriculum Connections

- Language Arts

Internet Skills

- Navigation

Critical Thinking Skills

- Research
- Information analysis

Student Outcomes

- Ability to articulate orally and in writing Internet searching skills, concepts, and strategies.
- Ability to navigate child-appropriate searching tools.
- Knowledge of keyword searching concepts.
- Knowledge of a particular form of poetry or a poet.

Extension Activities

- After students have located poetry information, ask them to write a poem based on their experience searching for the answer to the question.
- Ask one person from each group to write on the board the number of Websites they uncovered in their searches. Use the information for students to create graphs that visually detail the results found on each search tool. Ask students to write a paragraph explaining the differences demonstrated by the graphs.

Activity Procedure

1. Explain to students they are going to be researching poetry and poets on the Internet. Ask them to tell you what they already know about the topic and what they would like to know.

2. Distribute the activity sheet *Poetry Questions and Words*. Divide the class into groups and ask each group to come up with a poetry question based on what students said they wanted to learn about poetry.

3. Bring the class back together and ask each group to report on the questions that they developed. Ask the class to pick one question to which they all would like to find the answer.

4. Have all the students write down the question. Then ask them to circle the words they think are key to the topic. Facilitate a whole-class discussion in which students report on the words that they circled.

5. Ask students to brainstorm words that either mean the same thing as those that they circled or are another way of saying the same thing. (You might want to have students use a thesaurus to help them come up with synonyms for the topic they are brainstorming.) Examples of what they might come up with include:
   - poet
   - rhyme
   - rhyming
   - poet's name
   - name of a poem
   - haiku
   - poetry
   - verse

6. Engage the class in a discussion on how search tools work and why it's important to try to figure out what words and phrases to use in order to be successful at searching.

7. Have the whole class select two terms from the word list that they think will be good to use in an Internet search.

8. Demonstrate the basic features of **Yahooligans!** and **KidsClick!**

9. Divide the class into groups and assign each group one of these two search tools:
   - **Yahooligans!**—*www.yahooligans.com/*
   - **KidsClick!**—*www.kidsclick.org/*

10. Have each group search using the terms chosen by the class. Distribute the activity sheet *Words and What They Lead To* for groups to use to keep track of what they uncover as they try their searches. In particular ask students to pay attention to the number of Websites they find for each term and the type of infor-

mation that is available at each site. Distribute the activity sheet *Go with the Flow* and tell each group that one person should fill in the chart to show the steps they took in the search process.

11. After the groups have performed their initial searches, bring them back together to discuss how to pick useful resources from the list generated by a search. Distribute the *Working with the Results* activity sheet. Have the class brainstorm the different criteria they might use in selecting resources from a results list and record their final criteria on the activity sheet.

12. Have the teams return to their search lists and select resources based on the criteria on the *Working with the Results* activity sheet.

13. Have each group visit one of the sites they think will be useful.

14. Bring the class back together to discuss what they found using the different search tools. What is the same and what is different about using the different tools? What's the same and what's different about what they found using each tool? What conclusions can be drawn from this information?

Website Alternatives

The Websites listed on the following page may be substituted for **KidsClick!** or **Yahooligans!** when integrating searching skills into the classroom.

Searching Notes for Teachers

- If in a one-computer classroom with a projection system, once students brainstorm search terms and phrases, demonstrate the different searches to the entire class or to small groups. During the demonstration help students answer the questions on the activity sheet. Allow different students to type in the searches in the search tool. After the assignment is completed suggest that students try searching on their own, or in small groups, when they have time during the school day.

- At the third-grade level focus students on the category headings available on the main page of **Yahooligans!** and **KidsClick!** Start their search by helping them to see the connections between the categories and the sites listed within. Have students draw a Web of the subject headings found within one of the **KidsClick!** or **Yahooligans!** categories.

- At the fourth- and fifth-grade levels consider expanding the students' search into a Web quest. Assign roles to team members (poet, publisher, reader, and so on) and have each team member develop a search strategy based on his/her role and the type of information required for the person in that role.

Ask Jeeves for Kids

www.askjeevesforkids.com/

One of the most useful aspects of **Ask Jeeves for Kids** is the list of questions generated by a search. You can use this list to help students come up with other ways of posing their research question. **Ask Jeeves for Kids** is also a useful tool for help in coming up with keywords and phrases that might be used when searching with another search tool. Have students look carefully at the questions provided on the results list and write down any terms or phrases that might be useful when searching using another tool.

Internet Public Library Youth Division

www.ipl.org/youth/

Although the **Internet Public Library Youth Division** is not searchable, its subject heading structure is a good place to start students as they begin to think about how Internet search tools are organized. Ask students to figure out how to find poetry resources at the **Internet Public Library Youth Division**. Students might also draw a chart comparing the subject headings used in **Yahooligans!**, **KidsClick!**, and the **Internet Public Library Youth Division**.

Activity Sheet

Poetry Questions and Words

Student Name(s):

The question our group would like to answer is:

After the class talked about all the questions the groups were interested in having answered, the one the class decided on is:

The key words in our question are:

Words that mean the same thing as the important words in our question are:

Activity Sheet

Words and What They Lead To

Student Name(s):

Words we are searching for:

Name and address of the search tool we are going to use:
http://

Number of sites listed when we did our search:

This seems like **way too many**, **not enough**, or **just the right number** of sites for finding the information we need. Why?

If you retrieved a list of way too many sites or not enough sites, what ideas do you have for getting better results.

Activity Sheet

Go with the Flow

Student Name(s):

Fill in one rectangle for each step that you take in the search process.

Searching For:

Activity Sheet

Working with the Results

Student Name(s):

These are the criteria we are going to use to select resources on the search results list:

1.

2.

3.

4.

5.

6.

7.

8.

9.

10.

LESSON PLAN—DEVELOPING EFFECTIVE SEARCH STRATEGIES

Overview

Searching sometimes requires that students understand differences between search tools and know how to use Boolean operators to develop effective search strategies. This lesson uses Venn diagrams and set theory to help students learn about search tools and how Boolean searching works. The lesson focuses on the topic of roller coasters and presumes that students have already begun researching roller coasters using print materials.

Before Getting Started

Make sure you are familiar with the different search tools and how they work. Try out the searches students perform. This helps you get acquainted with the resources they might locate and the type of information available on the topic. Work with students on their preliminary research about roller coasters and start them thinking about the research process as it relates to books and the Internet.

Student Prerequisites

- Web navigation skills
- Beginning searching skills
- Preliminary information on roller coasters culled from books and magazines
- A list of questions students would like to have answered about the physics of roller coasters

Technology Requirements

- Individual or small group computer access
- Internet access
- Access to the World Wide Web

Lesson Sidebar 5 The Critical Thinking Connection—The Logic of Searching

If students become skilled at developing search strategies and understand how different search tools work, they will have a greater likelihood of being successful in their Web searching. As you work with students on Boolean searching techniques, have them articulate in as many ways as possible—through images, text, and spoken word—the principles of this type of searching. Thinking through the techniques in a variety of different ways, students have a better chance of understanding the logic behind the technique.

Activity Sheets

- *What We Want to Know*
- *In Words and Pictures*
- *How Search Tools Work*
- *Go With the Flow*
- *Finding the Sites*

Grade Level

- Grades 4 and 5

Curriculum Connections

- Math
- Science

Internet Skills

- Searching

Critical Thinking Skills

- Research
- Information analysis

Student Outcomes

- Ability to articulate orally and in writing Boolean searching techniques.
- Ability to develop and perform Boolean searches.
- Understanding of search tools, how they work, and differences between tools.
- Understanding of the differences between searching using a library catalog and using a Web-based search tool.
- Knowledge of the physics of roller coasters.

Extension Activities

- Give students Venn diagrams of searches and ask them to record what the diagrams show. Or, provide students with sentences describing searches and ask them to show the search in a Venn diagram.

- Have students build working models of roller coasters using the information they collected via their book and Web research.
- Ask students to write a booklet for other students on how to use search tools and how to develop Boolean searches.

Activity Procedure

1. Students begin their research by using library resources to find information on the physics of roller coasters. After the initial re search is completed, explain to students they are going to continue the process by looking for more information using Web-based search tools.

2. Distribute the activity sheet *What We Want To Know.* Have students record what they have learned so far about the physics of roller coasters in the "What We Know" column and questions they have about roller coasters in the "What We Want to Know" column. Explain that they will fill in the "What We Learned" column after they complete their Web searching.

3. As a whole class, brainstorm terms and phrases related to questions that students have about the physics of roller coasters. Some terms and phrases students might come up with include:
   - roller coasters
   - ride
   - amusement park
   - physics
   - coaster
   - coasters
   - carnival
   - fair

4. As a whole class, discuss the concepts behind Boolean searching. Key points to consider with students include:
   - Boolean theory uses what are called operators to create sets of information.
   - Boolean theory has much in common with set theory learned in elementary school math.
   - The most commonly used operators in search tools are "and," "or," "not."
   - **"And"** tells a search tool to display only those items that include all of the terms. So a search for "roller coasters" and "physics" returns a list of Web pages that include **both** the phrase "roller coaster" and the word "physics."
   - **"Or"** tells a search tool to display those items that include any of the terms used in the search. So a search for "roller coasters" or "physics" returns a list of Web pages that include **either** the phrase "roller coaster" **or** the word "physics."

- **"Not"** tells a search tool to display those items that include one term but not another. So a search for "roller coasters" not "physics" returns a list of Web pages that include the phrase "roller coaster" but not the word "physics."
- Each search tool may have different ways to do Boolean searching. It's a good idea to read the "Help" information at each tool before trying the search.

5. Divide the class into teams and distribute the activity sheet *In Words and Pictures* to each. Ask students to select two terms or phrases from the list generated and use those to develop three Boolean searches. They should use both a sentence and a Venn diagram to define their searches. For example, a sentence might be:

    Find Web pages that have information on "roller coasters" and "physics."

    The Venn diagram would look like this:

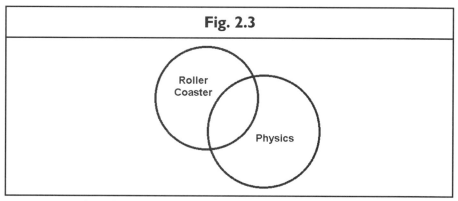

Fig. 2.3

6. Bring the class back together and inform the groups that each one will search for information on roller coasters using a different search tool. Let them know that when they are finished searching they will compare notes on what each group uncovered.

7. Demonstrate to the entire class how to use the different search tools. As you demonstrate the tools, facilitate a discussion about the differences between search engines and search directories. (See the information on search tools earlier in this unit.) Be sure to point out to students the "Help" section at each site.

8. Distribute the activity sheet *How Search Tools Work*. As you demonstrate the tools, have students record their notes about the how each of the tools works.

9. Assign each group a search tool to use. These might include:
    - **Alta Vista**—*www.altavista.com/*
    - **Excite**—*www.excite.com/*
    - **Google**—*www.google.com/*
    - **HotBot**—*www.hotbot.com/*
    - **Lycos**—*www.lycos.com/*

10. Have the groups try each of the searches they developed using the *In Words and Pictures* activity sheet. Ask one person in each group to record the searching process on the *Go with the Flow* activity sheet.

11. Ask each group to select at least five resources they found that they think will have useful information related to the topic they are searching. Have students fill out the *Finding the Sites* activity sheet as they select sites from the results list.

12. Bring the class back together to discuss the process of searching on the Internet. Ask them to articulate what they found, what they were surprised by, what was difficult, and what was easy. Have students fill in the final column of the *What We Want to Know* worksheet and ask them if there is information they still need to locate. If there is information that is still required, have students brainstorm methods they can use for finding the remaining information. Have them consider resources beyond books and Websites, including e-mail, magazines, and so on.

13. Finish the lesson by having students compare the search strategies and techniques they used for locating information using library resources and Web-based search tools.

The Logic of Searching Notes for Teachers
- In a one-computer classroom, have the entire class develop a joint search strategy, and use a computer projection system to demonstrate Boolean searching with a variety of search tools. If a projection system is not available, have each group work on a different part of the roller coaster physics research. While some students are looking for information in books, other students can be creating their Boolean searches, and other students can be performing their searches on the Web.
- At the third-grade level connect Boolean searching to set theory, which students learn in primary grade math classes. Instead of focusing students on the terms used for Boolean operators, work with them to develop sets by combining words and phrases and discussing which combinations will lead to the largest and smallest sets of results.
- At the fourth- and fifth-grade levels have students pick topics of interest and develop search strategies and Boolean searches. Challenge students to construct searches that will give them the most precise results. See what team can come up with a search strategy that generates the least number of useful results.

Activity Sheet		
What We Want to Know		
Student Name(s):		
What We Know	**What We Want to Know**	**What We Learned**

Activity Sheet

In Words and Pictures

Student Name(s):

The terms/phrases we are searching for are:

An **and** search with the terms/phrases in words and in picture. Write one of your terms in each circle and then color in the area of the diagram that represents **and**. Also write a sentence that explains your search.

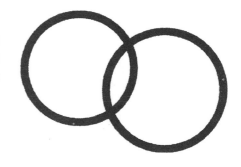

An **or** search with the terms/phrases in words and in picture. Write one of your terms in each circle and then color in the area of the diagram that represents **or**. Also write a sentence that explains your search.

A **not** search with the terms/phrases in words and in picture. Write one of your terms in each circle and then color in the area of the diagram that represents **not**. Also write a sentence that explains your search.

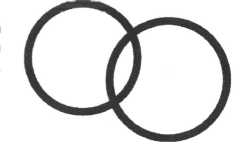

Activity Sheet		
How Search Tools Work		
Student Name(s):		
Search Tool Name	**URL**	**How It Works**

Activity Sheet

Go with the Flow

Student Name(s):

Fill in one diamond for each step that you take in the search process.

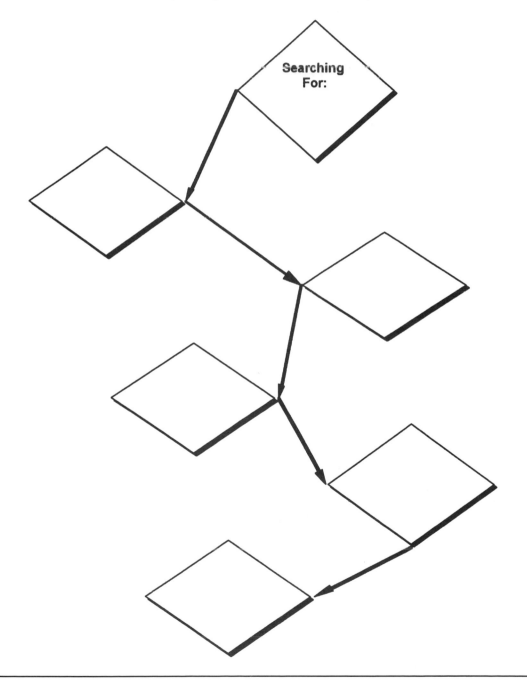

Activity Sheet
Finding the Sites Student Name(s):   Name and address of the search tool we are using: **http://**   The terms and/or phrases we are using in our search are: The sites listed look like they have **lots**, **some**, **no information** related to our topic: We think this because: Visit five sites. The names and addresses of five sites we think have the information we are looking for are: The title and Web address of our favorite one is: This is our favorite site because:

LESSON PLAN—EVALUATING WEBSITES

Overview

Students need to be able to evaluate the resources they find on the Web. This lesson asks students to critically look at the information they find on a Website to determine its authority and validity.

Before Getting Started

Become familiar with the sites used in this lesson—**KIDS Report**, *http://kids.library.wisc.edu/*, **The Electronic Zoo**, *http://netvet.wustl.edu/e-zoo.htm*, and **The Underground Railroad @ National Geographic**, *www.nationalgeographic.com/features/99/railroad/index.html*. Evaluate and review these sites yourself before you ask students to do the same thing. Think about the aspects of site evaluation that you think are the most important and be sure to point those out to students.

Student Prerequisites

- Web navigation skills

Technology Requirements

- Individual or small group computer access
- Internet access
- Access to the World Wide Web

Lesson Sidebar 6 The Critical Thinking Connection—Evaluation

When students evaluate Websites they need to consider many different aspects of the site in order to make a thorough and reasoned evaluation. By having students develop their own set of evaluation criteria you help them to examine and understand the important issues that need to be considered when looking at materials on the Web. When students look at Websites, they should realize they need to consider who is presenting the information, the purpose for the site, the accuracy of the information, and usefulness of the material presented. They should also consider issues of navigation and design and think about how easy it is to move around a site, how links are labeled, and if access is impeded by technology requirements of any kind.

Activity Sheets

- *What Makes a Good Website*
- *Our Own Evaluation*

Grade Level

- Grades 3 through 5

Curriculum Connections

- Social Science
- Language Arts

Internet Skills

- Navigation

Critical Thinking Skills

- Evaluation
- Information analysis

Student Outcomes

- Ability to develop criteria for Website evaluation.
- Ability to evaluate a Website.
- Ability to articulate orally and in writing criteria needed to successfully evaluate a Website.

Extension Activities

- Have students evaluate sites on topics of interest to them. Then they write reviews of the sites and publish the reviews either in print or electronic form.
- Have students compare the criteria they use for evaluating a Website to how they evaluate a book or magazine. Ask them to draw a chart or Web that shows the similarities and differences in the two types of evaluation.
- After students have created their own evaluation criteria, divide them into groups and have each group develop a presentation—with PowerPoint, Hyperstudio, or Kid Pix —on how to evaluate Websites.
- Have students create a flowchart, Web, or storyboard for the

pages on the **Underground Railroad @ National Geographic** Website in order to show connections between pages.

Activity Procedure

1. Explain to students they are going to be visiting a Website on the Underground Railroad and that their job is to decide if the site is one that they think includes useful information for learning about the Railroad.

2. Show students the **KIDS Report** Website, *http://kids.library.wisc.edu/*, and explain that the site provides reviews of Websites written by students. Look at some of the reviews and talk with students about the kind of information that is included in the reviews.

3. Show the class the **KIDS Report** criteria and facilitate a discussion about the different criteria. Select one of the sites evaluated at the **KIDS Report** and start a discussion about what makes a good Website. Point out the good and the bad qualities of the site viewed.

4. Distribute the activity sheet *What Makes a Good Website* and brainstorm a list of criteria that the students in the class would like to use to evaluate Websites themselves. Have students record their final criteria on the activity sheet.

5. As a whole class have students look at the **Electronic Zoo** site, *http://netvet.wustl.edu/e-zoo.htm*. Be sure to point out where you find the copyright date of the site and how you locate information about the author. While looking at the site, have students use the evaluation criteria they developed to evaluate the site.

6. Divide students into groups and have each group visit the **Underground Railroad @ National Geographic** Website, *www.nationalgeographic.com/features/99/railroad/index.html*. Distribute the activity sheet *Our Own Evaluation*. Tell the groups to use the criteria they created to evaluate the site. Make sure to point out to the students that they will want to look at all the different pieces of the site, not just the main pages. (For example, they will want to look at the "Timeline" section of the site.)

7. After the students have finished looking at the Website, bring the class back together for a discussion of their evaluation of the site. Ask students to report on their answers to the questions on the activity sheet. Make sure to have the students tell you why they answered the evaluation questions they way they did. If students disagree about the Website, set up a debate on the topic of the evaluation of the site.

Evaluation Notes for Teachers
- In a one-computer classroom, the entire lesson could be presented as a whole-class demonstration (if a computer projection system is available). As a whole class, look at a Website and ask students to consider their evaluation criteria and to determine the site's positive and negative qualities. If a computer projection system is unavailable, small groups of students could work on the computer portion of this lesson while other students are working on other aspects of the activity.
- At the third-grade level work with students to understand the concepts related to site ownership and authorship and how that has an impact on an evaluation. Make comparisons to printed materials wherever possible to help students understand the concepts.
- At the fifth-grade level extend the lesson to include evaluation of the quality of the text on the Website. Ask students if there are sections of the site they think need editing. Have students write their own text for one of the pages within the site.

Website Alternatives

The Websites listed below may be substituted for the **Underground Railroad @ National Geographic** site to teach evaluation skills within another content area.

FLEETKIDS (MATH)

www.fleetkids.com/

This Website is sponsored by Fleet Bank and includes activities for students to learn about a variety of mathematical and economic concepts. When evaluating this site make sure that students read the "About FleetKids" information. Ask students to see if they can figure out who the sponsor of the site is by looking at the "About" information and the URL. Make sure that students look at the different methods of navigating the site, using drop-down menus and text and image links, and ask them to consider the impact the navigation has on the evaluation of the site. Also, ask students to think about how they would gather information about the topic of math from this site and what they think is the purpose of the site.

THE GREAT PLANT ESCAPE (SCIENCE)

www.urbanext.uiuc.edu/gpe/index.html

At this site students solve mysteries to learn about plants. **The Great Plant Escape** is a good site to use for evaluating a site based on the navigational structure. As students evaluate **The Great Plant Escape** make sure they consider how the site is organized and what methods are available for getting from one mystery, or section, to another. Ask students to consider if they think the site is successful at teaching about plants.

INVENTION DIMENSION (SCIENCE)

http://web.mit.edu/afs/athena.mit.edu/org/i/invent/

Students learn about inventors and inventions at this site. As students evaluate this site, be sure to ask them to consider the navigational structure of the site. Ask older students to notice the host of the site and ask them to think about the importance of knowing that a well-known and respected institution of higher education provides this information.

MATH, BASEBALL, AND THE SAN FRANCISCO GIANTS (MATH)

www.kn.pacbell.com/wired/baseball/

When visiting this Website students learn math concepts within the framework of a San Francisco Giants baseball game. As students evaluate this site, make sure that they pay attention to the author of the site. Ask them to consider how much information on an author is necessary when evaluating a site. Also, ask students to think about the purpose of the site and if that purpose is fulfilled. Have them decide whether or not there is enough information presented at the site to learn math concepts.

MUSEUM OF WEB ART (ART)

www.mowa.org/

This site is a one-stop spot for viewing and learning about art on the Web. As students evaluate the **Museum of Web Art** site, make sure that they locate the "About MOWA" section of the site. See if they can figure out what the purpose of the site is and then ask them to determine if that purpose is met. Ask the students to consider the type of information presented at the site and what they think someone would learn by visiting the **Museum of Web Art**. In the "Kids Wing" students will have to enter a name and age. This provides a good opportunity to discuss issues of Internet safety as they relate to giving out information via a Website or e-mail.

THE OREGON TRAIL (HISTORY/SOCIAL SCIENCE)

www.isu.edu/~trinmich/Oregontrail.html

This site includes facts about the trail, diary entries, and information about points of interest along the trail. As students evaluate the site, have them locate information about the authors of the site and ask them to consider the importance of the author's credentials in their evaluation. How they would locate information on the site and do they think that the information provided would be useful to them?

SCHOOLHOUSE ROCK (MATH)

http://genxtvland.simplenet.com/SchoolHouseRock/

This Website is a companion to the television program of the same name. When evaluating this site, make sure that students consider why there are two versions available—a "High Graphics Version" and a "Low Graphics Version." Divide the class so that some of the students evaluate the "High Graphics Version" and some evaluate the "Low Graphics Version." Then bring the class together and have the students compare their evaluations of the two versions.

TALES OF WONDER (LANGUAGE ARTS)

http://members.xoom.com/darsie/tales/index.html

This Website provides access to folk tales from around the world. As students evaluate this site, make sure they consider issues of currency and authority. Ask students if it matters if the site has not been updated in quite a long time. This is a good discussion to have since not all content needs to be updated. You could discuss with students what type of content should be updated regularly and what type of content does not need regular updating. Also, make sure that students consider the authorship and sponsorship of the site.

TREASURE ISLAND (LANGUAGE ARTS)

www.ukoln.ac.uk/services/treasure/

At this Website you will find Information about the novel and the author of *Treasure Island*, along with complementary activities for students. As students evaluate the **Treasure Island** site, make sure they take a look at the different ways to navigate (text and images) and the author and sponsor of the site. Have older students look at both the frames and the no frames versions of the site and consider the differences between the two. Make sure they look at the links section in both frames and no frames versions. While in the frames version, ask students to see if the URL of the site changes when they access a resource from another site. Ask students to consider the impact of using frames on a visitor's experience at the site.

You Be the Historian (History/Social Science)

http://americanhistory.si.edu/hohr/springer/index.htm

At this Website students learn history by trying to figure out what life was like for a family 200 years ago. As students evaluate this Website, be sure that they note who hosts the site and that they consider the impact of that information on their evaluation of the site. Ask students to look for information about the host. Also, ask them to see if they can find an author of **You Be the Historian** and consider whether or not in this instance it is essential to have the name of the author to evaluate the site effectively.

Activity Sheet

What Makes a Good Website?

Student Name(s):

This is what we are going to look for on the Websites that we evaluate:

1.

2.

3.

4.

5.

6.

7.

8.

We think the most important part of evaluating Websites is:

We think this is important because:

Activity Sheet

Our Own Evaluation

Student Name(s):

This is the name and address of the Website we are evaluating:

In the left column write the criteria you are using to evaluate the site. On the right record your thoughts on how well the site meets the criteria and why.

Evaluation Criteria	Website Success

Rate this site

1	2	3	4	5
Worst site ever!	Has a couple of good things.	Pretty good, but could be better.	Not bad, but not perfect either.	Best site ever created!

Why did you give this site that rating?

LESSON PLAN—ANALYZING RESULTS

Overview

In this lesson students search several different e-commerce sites to locate the lowest price of a book. Students learn how to use a price comparison tool, find out the differences in the cost of books in different formats, calculate differences in prices, and brainstorm reasons that a book might have several different prices.

Before Getting Started

Visit the **DealTime** site, *http://media.dealtime.com/books.html*, used in this lesson. Search for authors and titles that are familiar to students. Note that you can search for author, title, keyword, or ISBN. Students will probably be searching by author or title. The more specific students can be with the title or the author, the easier it will be for them to compare prices. Become familiar with the information that is generated through a search and how to read the screen that displays search results.

Student Prerequisites

- Knowledge of Web navigation skills
- Ability to perform simple searches

Technology Requirements

- Individual or small group computer access
- Internet access
- Access to the World Wide Web

Lesson Sidebar 7 The Critical Thinking Connection—Price Comparison Sites

Students learn a great deal about searching, as well as mathematics, by using price comparison sites. As they navigate the **DealTime** site, make sure to point out the different search options available. Ask students to consider why they would select one option over another. As students view the results list generated by their search, have them pay attention to the type of information provided in the list. Ask them to read the information carefully and then to articulate their decision-making process for choosing one item on the list over another.

Activity Sheets

- *How Much Does It Cost?*
- *Playing with the Numbers?*

Grade Level

- Grades 3 through 5

Curriculum Connections

- Math
- Language Arts

Internet Skills

- Navigation
- Searching

Critical Thinking Skills

- Research
- Information analysis

Student Outcomes

- Ability to articulate orally and in writing reasons for differences in the prices of items available for purchase.
- Ability to articulate orally and in writing methods for searching.
- Knowledge of how to search a Website.
- Understanding of basic mathematical and economic principles related to item costs.

Extension Activity

- Join the **Global Grocery List Project,** *http://landmark-project.com/ggl/.* For this project students visit the grocery store to record the price of a variety of items. After collecting the data submit it to the **Global Grocery List Project** Website and then compare the prices at the local grocery store with the prices at grocery stores around the world.

Activity Procedure

1. Ask students if they know anyone who buys things online. Explain to the class that they will be searching a Website to find out the cost of a book at several online stores.

2. As a whole class, brainstorm a list of book titles and authors that students would recommend to a friend. If students can't remember the exact name of an author or the title of a book, suggest that they see if they can find it in the library catalog. (Remember that the more specific students can be with an author or title, the more successful they will be in their search.)

3. Select one of the titles or authors from the list created by students. Visit the **DealTime** site, *http://media.dealtime.com/ books.html*, and show students how to perform a search and read the results screen. Make sure to point out they will want to look carefully at each item on the results list to make sure it's the book they are looking for. Mention that both the author and title have to be the same as that of the book for which they are searching.

4. Divide students into groups and distribute the *How Much Does It Cost* activity sheet. Present students with the following scenario:

   > A friend's birthday is coming up and you have decided to give him a book as a present. However, money is tight and it's important to find a copy of the book at the lowest price possible. You need to search the Web and find a version of the book that you can afford.

5. Assign each group one title or author to search for at the **DealTime** site. Before they start searching ask each group to predict what they think will be the lowest and highest price of the book for which they are searching. Each group should record that price on the activity sheet.

6. Have each group perform its search and write down each book price listed. Make sure to point out to the students that they should write down the prices only for the books they are sure are by the same author and have the same title as the book for which they are searching. Also mention that they should write down the format of the book, hardcover, paperback, and so forth, along with the price.

7. After students have finished finding the prices, bring the class back together to compare notes on the cost of the books. Ask them to brainstorm reasons why the different editions of a book

Searching Price Comparison Sites Notes for Teachers

- In a one-computer classroom, demonstrate to students how to search the **DealTime** site. Ask students to make predictions about the cost of a book for which they would like to search and then either perform the search for the class using a projection system or have students access the site individually or in small groups throughout the day. As students search the site, have them write down the prices and record their findings in a central location in the classroom. When all the findings are gathered, have students compare the information and develop charts and graphs that demonstrate the differences in pricing.
- At the third-grade level use this lesson to reinforce basic searching concepts. Be sure to explain the differences between searching by author and title, and give students a chance to explore the differences between the basic search options. Also focus on the differences in format and why an item in one format would cost more or less than an item in another format.
- At the fifth-grade level ask different groups of students to search different shopping comparison sites. After the searching is completed ask students to compare the prices found on the sites and discuss the differences between the comparison sites.

have a different price. Also, have the students discuss what they liked and didn't like about searching at the **DealTime** site.

8. Have the students return to their groups to start working on math calculations related to the book prices they uncovered. Distribute the activity sheet *Playing with the Numbers* and ask students to figure out the different calculations. Give the groups graphing paper and have them graph the different costs of the books. (You could also use graphing software if available.)

9. After students have completed the calculations, bring the class back together to compare the price differences that they discovered.

Website Alternatives

The Websites listed below may be substituted for **DealTime** and may be used to compare the prices of items.

BOTTOM DOLLAR

www.bottomdollar.com/

C|NET SHOPPER

www.shopper.com/

MYSIMON

www.mysimon.com/

PRICESCAN.COM

www.pricescan.com/

Activity Sheet	
How Much Does It Cost?	

Student Name(s):

The book and/or author we are searching for is:

We think the lowest price will be:	**We think the highest price will be:**
These are the different prices for the book:	**The format of each book is:**
1.	1.
2.	2.
3.	3.
4.	4.
5.	5.
6.	6.
7.	7.
8.	8.
9.	9.

Activity Sheet

Playing with the Numbers

Student Name(s):

The author and title of the book we searched for is:

Draw a chart (or charts) to graphically display one or more of the following:

- The highest price of the book
- The lowest price of the book
- The amount of money you will save by buying the book at the lowest price
- The average price of the book
- The difference between the highest price and what you predicted as the highest price
- The difference between the lowest price and what you predicted as the lowest price

WHERE DO I FIND OUT MORE ABOUT THE WEB?

This is a list of resources mentioned in this unit, along with other materials on how the Web works and ways in which you can integrate it into the classroom.

Alta Vista

www.altavista.com/

This is a search engine.

America's Story at America's Library

www.americaslibrary.gov/

The Library of Congress provides information on people and events throughout America's history.

DealTime—Books

http://media.dealtime.com/books.html

Search for a book by author or title and find out what it costs at different e-commerce sites.

Education World

www.education-world.com

Visit **Education World** to find lesson plans on integrating the Web into the curriculum or read reviews of Websites.

Excite

www.excite.com/

This is a search engine.

Global Grocery List Project

http://htlandmark-project.com/ggl/

After students collect data on the price of items in the grocery store, they can compare local prices with those in stores around the country or the world.

Google

www.google.com/

This is a search engine.

HotBot

www.hotbot.com/

This is a search engine.

Kids Books at About.com

http://kidsbooks.about.com/kids/kidsbooks/

This site has articles and links to resources on books for kids.

KidsClick!

www.kidsclick.org/

This is a search directory, created and maintained by librarians, of various kids' sites.

KIDS Report

http://kids.library.wisc.edu/

Websites are reviewed by kids from elementary school through high school.

Lewis & Clark @ National Geographic.com

www.nationalgeographic.com/lewisclark/index.html

Students join Lewis and Clark on their expedition at this Website.

Librarians' Index to the Internet

www.lii.org/

This is a search directory, created and maintained by librarians, that includes sites for children and adults.

Lycos

www.lycos.com/

This is a search engine.

Mighty m&m Math Project

http://mighty-mm-math.caffeinated.org/main.htm

Students compare what's in the contents of their bag of m&ms with those opened in classrooms around the country.

NickNacks Telecollaborate

http://home.talkcity.com/academydr/nicknacks/

Learn about telecollaborative projects and learn how to create your own.

The Underground Railroad @ National Geographic

www.nationalgeographic.com/features/99/railroad/index.html

Kids take on the role of slaves and decide whether or not to escape on the Underground Railroad.

The WebQuest Page

http://edweb.sdsu.edu/webquest/webquest.html

Find out how to create a Web quest for your classroom, or use a Web quest that another teacher has already created.

Yahoo!

www.yahoo.com/

This is a large search directory of sites for children and adults.

Yahooligans!

www.yahooligans.com/

The companion to Yahoo!, this is a search directory of kid-appropriate sites.

BASIC WEB GLOSSARY

Browser

The software that enables users to access the World Wide Web, including still and moving images and sounds.

Code (see also HTML, Source)

When a Web page is created, the author uses a series of HTML codes that inform the browser how the content of the page should be displayed.

Home

The Web page that is designated in the user's browser as the page to access every time the browser is opened or when the "home" button is selected.

Home Page

The main page of a Website.

HTML (Hypertext Markup Language)

A programming language used to create basic Web pages.

Hyperlink

A word, sound, or image on a Web page that, when selected, leads to another word or image on the same or a different page.

Internet Explorer (see also Browser)

A piece of software that allows users to access the features of the Web.

Links (see Hyperlink)

Netscape Navigator (see also Browser)

A piece of software that allows users to access the features of the Web.

Search Directory

A database of Websites usually organized into subject categories.

Search Engine

An index of Websites that is searchable by keywords and phrases.

Source (see also Code, HTML)

When looking at a Web page, a visitor can view the code (sometimes referred to as the source code) that was used to define how the content of the page should be displayed.

URL (Uniform Resource Locator)

The address of a Website.

Web Page

A single page on a topic, usually part of a larger Website.

Website

A collection of pages on a particular topic.

World Wide Web

The collection of sites on the Internet connected via hyperlinks. Commonly referred to as "the Web."

Unit 3

Exploring E-mail

The most popular function of the Internet is e-mail. People use it to find old friends, communicate for business, and write letters to family members. E-mail is relatively easy to use and almost anyone can get an account using a free e-mail service. Once you know the basics, sending and receiving e-mail messages is simply accomplished. In this unit you'll find out how e-mail works, what are special features of some e-mail packages, and how to integrate e-mail into student writing and research.

WHAT IS E-MAIL?

Consider the path the mail you get in your postal mailbox takes every day. Imagine a friend is going to send you a letter:

- First she writes the letter.
- Then she puts it in an envelope and adds the address.
- Then she puts the addressed envelope in a mailbox.
- The post office takes over and sorts the letter so it will travel the correct route to the local post office that delivers your mail.
- A letter carrier brings the letter to your mailbox, which you open sometime during the day to read your mail.

The same types of steps happen with an e-mail message:

- First, someone decides to send you an e-mail message.
- He writes the message and adds your e-mail address. (In both

e-mail and postal mail a person needs to have an address and the sender needs to know the address in order for the mail to be delivered.)

- When the sender selects the "send" button, he sends the message to his post office—the mail service provider who handles his e-mail transactions.
- The provider then routes the message to the recipient's provider, who is responsible for delivering it to the recipient's e-mail mailbox.
- In order for the recipient to receive and read the message he has to open his e-mail box.

Some people wonder where an e-mail message lives before it is accessed by the recipient. It lives on the e-mail provider's server, which is just like the post office in this case, until the recipient asks to see her mail. When a person registers for an e-mail account, she is given space on the provider's mail server. This is where the mail is held until she opens up the mailbox by clicking the "Check Mail" button.

To send and receive e-mail, a person has to have an e-mail address and access to a mail server. Many free e-mail services are available that provide people with both of these components. When a person registers for an e-mail account, she also receives an e-mail address. An e-mail address is made up of two parts. The first part is the username of the owner of the address and the second part is the name of the server where the e-mail lives.

When registering for an e-mail address, it's important to try to create a username that can be easily remembered both by you and the people who will be sending you e-mail. Often when registering for

---

Fig. 3.1   Anatomy of an E-mail Address

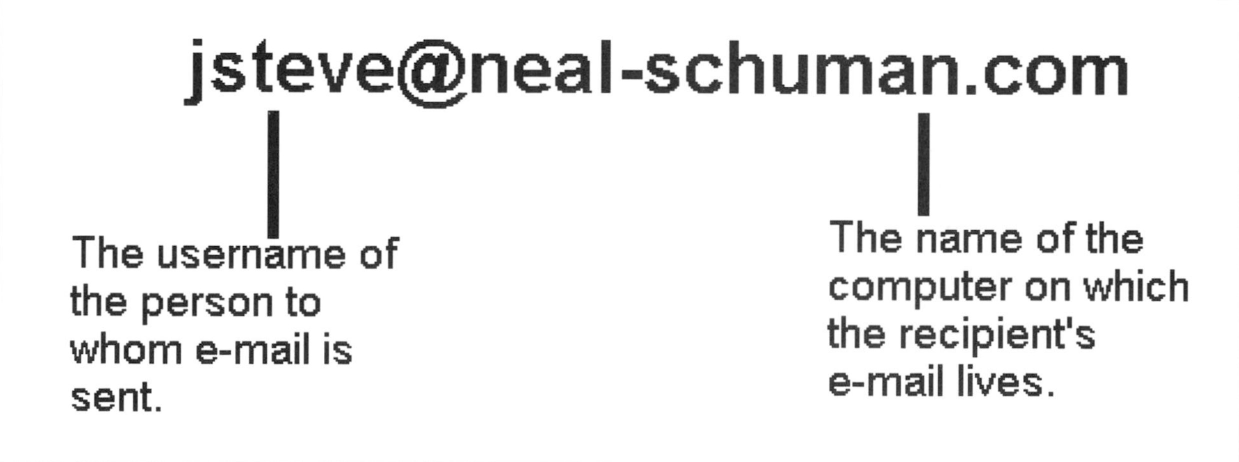

jsteve@neal-schuman.com

The username of the person to whom e-mail is sent.

The name of the computer on which the recipient's e-mail lives.

free e-mail services, common usernames—first name and last name, first initial and last name, and so forth—are already taken by one of the hundreds of other users registered for the service. If that's the case, try to develop something unique but which will still be easy for friends, colleagues, and family to remember.

WHAT IS A MAILING LIST? (ALSO KNOWN AS "LISTSERV")

A mailing list is a free subscription-based resource that enables people to talk to each other about a mutual topic of interest. Mailing lists exist on a wide variety of topics for both children and adults. These include topics such as integrating technology in the elementary classroom, pets, and hobbies. If it's a topic that people are interested in, you can be pretty certain that there's a mailing list about that topic.

A mailing list is run by a piece of computer software. The software keeps track of who has subscribed to the list and informs the computer where the list lives and what to do with messages it receives. This is how it works:

- You subscribe to a list by sending an e-mail (or submitting a Web-based form) to the computer with a message saying you want to subscribe.
- When the message is received and processed, you are added to the list of subscribers.
- Then, whenever any subscriber sends a message to the list, it is automatically sent to you.
- If you reply to the message, it is sent to everyone on the list, or if you send an original message to the list, it is sent to all of the subscribers.

Tile.net and **Listz** are two services that provide searchable access to information about mailing lists. If you want to know if there is a mailing list on a topic that you or your students are interested in, you can search either of these resources to see what's available. **Tile.net** and **Listz** also provide you with the address that you need in order to subscribe to a mailing list. Without that address you won't be added to the database of subscribers.

When you subscribe to a mailing list, you will receive an e-mail message with information and the "rules" of the list. It's important to keep this message. If you ever want to know how to remove yourself from the list or need to know how to get help on using the list, you'll find that information in the introductory message.

WHAT CAN I DO WITH E-MAIL?

What makes e-mail so exciting and useful to children and adults is the instantaneousness of the medium. In most cases, it doesn't take days for someone to receive and respond to an e-mail message. What often happens is that a message is sent and during that same day the person who received the message responds. E-mail isn't exactly instantaneous but it is quicker than sending a letter via postal mail, waiting for it to be delivered, and then waiting for the recipient to read and respond to it (by using postal mail once again.)

E-mail can be used by students to communicate with experts in a particular field of study. It can also be used to communicate with students in other schools or classrooms to learn about their lives and communities. Students can also use e-mail in collaborative writing lessons. (The lesson plans included in this unit cover these types of e-mail uses.)

When teaching students about using e-mail it's important to instruct them on more than the mechanics of sending a message:

- Remember to discuss with them language arts skills inherent in writing an articulate and understandable message.
- Before students send a message to an expert, make sure students carefully edit their message.
- This is a good time to teach students questioning and editing skills so they know when they send their message that their question is asked in a way that the recipient will understand and be able to respond appropriately.

When you are in the planning stages of integrating e-mail with students, you'll want to think about how best to organize the project and student e-mail access:

- Is each student going to have his or her own e-mail account and address or are the students going to be using a single address created by an adult?
- If students are not going to be able to access the e-mail messages in their own personal accounts, how are the messages going to be relayed to them?
- How often are students going to be able to access the e-mail to look for responses to their messages and reply to the messages that they receive?
- If access is going to be limited, it's a good idea to let the person students are communicating with know in advance. That way he or she won't be wondering why a response from students hasn't arrived.

Fig 3.2   ePals Logo

When looking for experts for students to communicate with, you'll want to make sure to check on the authority and reliability of the expert. **Ask A+ Locator** and **Ask an Expert** are two services on the Web that connect researchers with experts from various fields. These services are a good starting place for locating reputable experts. If you are planning to have students communicate with an expert, it's a good idea to e-mail the expert ahead of time and make sure that she will be able to respond to the messages students are going to send. (Similarly if you are going to have students send messages to a mailing list, check with the mailing list administrator to see if student messages are accepted by the list.)

If you are interested in connecting children to e-mail pen pals, take a look at **ePALS.com**. Once you have registered with **ePALS** you create a profile for your family, school, or library. You can search the **ePALS** database to find children in a particular part of the world with whom students can communicate. Or you can search the database for a specific topic students are studying to locate others studying the same content area. **ePALS** also provides free e-mail hosting, so if you are looking for an e-mail service provider, you can use **ePALS** for that as well.

E-mail is a powerful tool for teaching children writing and research skills. You'll find ideas on how to do that in the following lessons.

LESSON PLAN—USING E-MAIL IN RESEARCH

Overview

In this lesson children access the Web to find out who to e-mail to get information about one of the United States. Children e-mail an expert to get answers to questions on the state they are studying. (This lesson plan uses the example of a unit of study on the United States—other topics along with e-mail and Web resources can be substituted.)

Before Getting Started

Before you ask children to visit the official Website for a state, consider visiting the sites yourself. Make initial contact with people or agencies in each state in order to make sure that e-mail from students is accepted.

Student Prerequisites

- Preselection of a state to research
- Preliminary state research
- Basic knowledge of Web navigation skills

Technology Requirements

- Individual or small group computer access
- Access to e-mail software or Web-based e-mail
- Internet access
- Access to the World Wide Web

Lesson Sidebar 8   The Critical Thinking Connection—E-mailing Experts

When communicating via e-mail students need to consider several different issues. These relate to both the form of communication and the authority and reputability of an e-mail author. Develop methods for helping students think about the differences between e-mail and face-to-face communication. Ask students to design strategies for making up for these differences when communicating via e-mail. Also work with students to develop skills for ascertaining the reliability and authority of the person they are contacting. Develop a list of criteria for students to use in determining if the person with whom they are communicating is likely to be able to provide them with appropriate and accurate information.

Activity Sheets

- *Coming Up with the Questions*
- *Coming Up with the Answers*
- *E-mail Message Template*
- *Thank You and Follow-Up Message Template*

Grade Level

- Grades 3 through 5

Curriculum Connections

- Language Arts
- History/Social Science
- E-mail and Research Skills

Internet Skills

- Navigation
- E-mail

Critical Thinking Skills

- Information analysis
- Research

Student Outcomes

- Ability to articulate orally and in writing the components of an e-mail message.
- Knowledge of facts about the United States.
- Understanding of how to phrase a question.

Extension Activities

- Ask each group of students to locate the state they researched on a map and calculate the mileage between the state where they live and the state they researched.
- Divide the students into pairs. Have each pair interview each other about the state they researched. Then have the students report to the whole class what they learned in the interviews.
- Ask students to make a list of what they think is the same and what is different about the state where they live and the state

they researched. Have students create graphic organizers (for example, storyboards, flowcharts, or Webs) that visually demonstrate the differences.

Activity Procedure

1. Ask students as a whole class to brainstorm the information they would like to find out about their state. Depending on the state, teams might ask different kinds of questions. Talk about how to phrase questions to get an appropriate answer and how to know if you have asked a question that will elicit the information needed.

2. Explain to students how they can visit the official Website for each state. (Each state's official Web address has the same format—*www.state.twoletterabbreviation.us/*—so the Web address for Louisiana would be *www.state.la.us/*.) Then visit a state Website to show students the type of information available and how to find the appropriate e-mail address for sending a message to a state agency.

3. Explain to the students they will be asking their questions, via e-mail, of someone who lives and/or works in the state. Distribute the activity sheets *Coming Up with the Questions, Coming Up with the Answers,* and *E-mail Message Template.* Go over the activity sheets with the students and ask if they have any questions.

4. Divide students into small groups. In these groups they should decide the questions they want to ask of an official representative of the state they are studying. They should use the *E-mail Message Template* activity sheet to draft an e-mail message explaining who they are, why they are writing, and what questions they developed.

5. Teams should then visit the Website for the state they are researching. Have each team find the appropriate person or agency they will send their e-mail message to. Then have each group type the message they previously created into an e-mail program and send the message to the person or agency they selected. (Make sure to have students proofread and edit the message before they send it.)

6. Check the e-mail on a regular basis to collect answers. Teams might want to print out the answers and draft follow-up messages if they have more questions. Each team should send a thank-you message even if they don't have more questions to ask. Distribute the *Thank You E-mail Message Template* for students to use.

7. After the teams are satisfied with the answers they received,

E-mailing Experts Notes for Teachers

- If in a one-computer classroom, consider having the entire class work on researching their home state (or another state) together. Students would develop an e-mail message that would be sent by the whole class. Alternatively, students could work on different aspects of their state research at different times. For example, some students would visit the library to use print or electronic resources for locating information, while others would use the classroom computer to access the messages of the person to whom they will e-mail their questions.
- At the third- and fourth-grade levels inform students that a good place to start to locate the information they are looking for is probably the tourism section of the Website. Brainstorm terms that might be used on a Website in place of the word "tourism." For example, "vacation," "travel," "visit," and "chamber of commerce" might be link labels for tourism information on the site. Once students locate the tourism section of the site, help them find the appropriate person to e-mail with their questions.
- At the fifth-grade level, as students find the e-mail address of the person they are going to ask their questions, begin a discussion on the anatomy of an e-mail address. Have students compare the e-mail address with the address of the state Website.

bring the class back together to discuss the kinds of information successfully gathered via e-mail. Ask students to think about whether they uncovered the kinds of answers they expected and if they need to do more research using a different tool (books, magazines, and so forth).

8. Have teams complete research on the state they are studying, then each team presents an oral report about the state they studied and the process they used to gather information.

Website Alternatives

The following Websites listed may be substituted for the state Websites to integrate e-mail and questioning skills into the classroom. (Please note some of these sites use an online form for submitting questions to experts. You will want to explain to students that the form is sent to the expert in a method similar to e-mail and that responses will be received via e-mail.)

ASK A *MAYFLOWER* EXPERT (HISTORY/SOCIAL SCIENCE)

http://members.aol.com/calebj/mailto.html

This site includes passenger lists, a history of the *Mayflower*, and information about the ship's crew. In the introduction to this section of the Website, the author notes that his records do not go beyond 1720. This can help start a discussion with students about the questions they can ask that fit within the time frame of the author's knowledge base. As this service is a part of someone's personal Website on the *Mayflower*, you can discuss how to find out if the expert is reputable and why it's important to check someone's authority before asking for information.

HISTORY IN THE NATIONAL PARK SERVICE (HISTORY/SOCIAL SCIENCE, SCIENCE)

www.cr.nps.gov/history/askhist.htm

Experts on topics including Alaskan history, Native American history, and the Civil War are accessible through this National Park Service page. When working with students to e-mail one of the experts, begin at the first page of the site. Discuss what the National Park Service does. When you access the page for locating experts, have students consider why these experts are available via the National Park Service.

MADSCINET (SCIENCE)

www.madsci.org/

Before contacting an expert, search the **MadSciNet** archives with students to determine if their question has already been asked and answered. Take advantage of the archive search to discuss what types of questions other people asked, how other questions were phrased, and what answers were received. When students are ready to ask their own questions, show them all the pieces of the form and explain how selecting the appropriate options will help to ensure that their question is sent to the expert best suited to answer.

MATH CENTRAL—QUANDRIES AND QUERIES SERVICES (MATH)

http://MathCentral.uregina.ca/QQ/index.html#TOT

The "Quandries and Queries Services" section of the **Math Central** site provides different avenues for submitting a math question to an expert (found via the "Submit a Question" link). Before students write their question for submission to "Quandries and Queries," show them the different communication avenues outlined on the page and discuss the differences among them and why someone might choose one technique over another. As with **MadSciNet,** searching the "Quandries and Queries" database prior to writing and submitting a question will help students get a sense of how to successfully phrase questions.

Activity Sheet

Coming Up with the Questions

Student Name(s):

We are interested in finding out about (name of state):

The address of the official Website is:

We know this about our state	We want to learn these things about our state	In order to learn what we want to know about our state, we are going to ask these questions

The name and e-mail address of the person we are going to contact to find out about the state is:

We selected this person because:

We found information about this person in this section of the state Website:

Activity Sheet

Coming Up with the Answers

Student Name(s):

We know this about our state	We want to learn these things about our state	In order to learn what we want to know about our state, we are going to ask these questions

How are you going to find out the answers to the rest of your questions? Are you going to send another e-mail message to the same person, send a message to a different person, look in books or magazines, search the Internet?

The reason we are going to find the rest of the information this way is:

Activity Sheet

E-mail Message Template

Dear _____:

We are students in the ___ grade at _____ School. We are learning about the United States and would like to ask you a few questions about your state. These are our questions:

The e-mail address where you can send the answers to our questions is:

_____.

Thank you for helping us with our research.

Sincerely,
(names of students)

Activity Sheet

Thank You and Follow-Up Message Template

Dear _____:

Thank you for answering our questions about your state. We appreciate the time you took to help us with our research. Some of your answers made us think of other questions to ask. These are:

Thank you again for your help in our research.

Sincerely,
(names of students)

LESSON PLAN—COMMUNICATING WITH E-PALS

Overview

In this lesson children write messages to students in another part of the country using the **ePALS** Website for connecting with other students. The same lesson can be used a different e-pal service or with e-mail addresses accessed without a service. This lesson focuses on communicating with students who are studying the Middle Ages. However, it could be modified for a variety of other topics, including geography and world cultures.

Before Getting Started

Before starting the lesson register for the **ePALS** service, *www.epals.com/*. Create a profile for your classroom, library, or family. Become familiar with how **ePALS** works and search the descriptions for a classroom, library, or family that studies the Middle Ages. When you find a class with whom you would like students to communicate, contact the teacher, librarian, or parent to set up the structure for the lesson and the e-mail communication. Decide how often the class will send messages and set a general schedule for replying to the e-mail messages.

Student Prerequisites

- Beginning understanding of how to use e-mail and how e-mail works
- Web navigation skills
- Beginning Middle Ages research

Technology Requirements

- Individual or small group computer access

Lesson Sidebar 9 The Critical Thinking Connection—E-pals

As students communicate with their e-pals, make sure to start them thinking about the accuracy and authority of the information being exchanged. Talk with students about how they and their e-pals gather facts about the Middle Ages and what might happen to a fact when it is communicated to another person via e-mail. Use the e-pals communication to get students thinking about communication styles and the differences between asking a question and getting an answer when using e-mail and another form of communication.

- Internet access
- Access to the World Wide Web
- E-mail program, either via the Web or e-mail software

Activity Sheets

- *Let's Introduce Ourselves*
- *Questions About the Middle Ages*
- *Thanks for Working with Us Template*

Grade Level

- Grades 3 through 5

Curriculum Connections

- Language Arts
- History/Social Science

Internet Skills

- Navigation
- E-mail

Critical Thinking Skills

- Information analysis
- Research

Student Outcomes

- Familiarity with the components of an e-mail message.
- Knowledge of various facets of the Middle Ages.
- Understanding of how to ask a question.

Extension Activities

- Ask students to locate on a map the city where the students they are communicating with live. Then calculate the distance between your school and the school of the other class.
- Have students write a story about what it's like to live where they live and e-mail it to the students in the other classroom.

- Write a story together with the students in the other class. One class starts the story and e-mails it to the other class. Then each class adds a paragraph to the story until it is complete. After the story is finished, each class can edit and illustrate it. The final version can be sent as an e-mail attachment to the other classroom.
- Have students draw a map of the town where they live and, after scanning it, send it to the students in the other classroom.
- E-mail the students in the other class to find out specific details of the climate, geology, geography, and so forth, of their town.

Activity Procedure

1. Show students the **ePALS** Website. Explain to them how the site works and demonstrate how you searched for a classroom, or family, to find one with whom the students would communicate.

2. Inform students that the class they are going to communicate with has also been studying the Middle Ages. Explain that they are going to be sending these students e-mail messages with questions and thoughts about the Middle Ages. The first thing they will do is send an introductory message to the other class to tell a little bit about themselves.

3. Distribute the activity sheet *Let's Introduce Ourselves*.

4. Divide the class into small groups and have each group make a list of the things they want to tell the other class about themselves. Have the groups record the information on the activity sheet along with a draft paragraph of the e-mail message they are going to send.

5. Bring the class together and ask each group to report on the information they have on their list.

6. As a whole class select the information that students think should be in the introductory message and develop the full text for the message.

7. Demonstrate to students how to send an e-mail message to the **ePALS** classroom. Send the class message and then let students know you will check to see when the class has sent a reply to your students.

8. After the message is sent tell students about the next part of the project—developing a list of questions they would like to ask the other classroom about the Middle Ages. Distribute the activity sheet *Questions About the Middle Ages*.

9. Divide the class into small groups again and have each group

come up with three questions they would like to have the other class answer about the Middle Ages. Have students record their questions on the activity sheet.

10. Bring the class back together to discuss the questions each group came up with. Facilitate a discussion on what makes a good question and on ways that questions can be phrased so they can be more easily answered.

11. Tell each group they will send a message to students in the **ePALS** class. However, before they do that they have to write out the message along with their questions to make sure there are no grammatical or typographical errors.

12. Have each group record their draft message on the activity sheet. Then have each group type their message into the e-mail template at **ePALS**, proofread the message, and send it. Inform the students you will be checking the e-mail regularly to see if they have received a response.

13. When students receive a response to their e-mail message, ask them how they can check to see if the answers to the questions submitted are correct. Then have the students submit follow-up questions or information to the **ePALS** class.

14. When students have finished communicating about the Middle Ages, inform them that the last part of this project is to send "e-cards" to the students in the other class. ("E-card" is a generic term for a card sent electronically.) Brainstorm with the entire class the type of message they would like to include in this card. Distribute the *Thanks for Working with Us Template*

E-pal Notes for Teachers

- If in a one-computer classroom, groups of students can send their messages to e-pals at different times of the day. Or, your class can communicate with the other class as an entire group, sending one message at a time from the whole class instead of from small groups of students.

- At the third-grade level concentrate on first communication with e-pals on topics related to the students' day-to-day lives. Have students send e-mail to ask about the community in which the other students live and to find out about the interests of the other students. Give third graders opportunities to compare their own lives and community with lives and community of the e-pals. Also, provide them with chances for telecollaborating on creative projects such as writing a short story together.

- At the fifth-grade level give students the chance to do their own searching for a classroom in which to find e-pals. Demonstrate to students how the classroom search feature of the **ePals** site works. Brainstorm terms to use in an **ePals** search and criteria to use in selecting a classroom with which to communicate.

activity sheet to give students an idea of what they might write in the thank-you message.

15. After the ideas are generated, students should return to their small groups. Have each group write the message they would like to send to the students in the other class. Then show each group how to send an "e-card" via the **ePALS** site. When they are finished, let them know that you will check the e-mail on a regular basis to see if they have received a reply.

16. After the project is completed, have the whole class talk about what they learned about the Middle Ages by communicating with the other class. Ask them, also, what they learned about the other students via the e-mail communication.

Activity Sheet

Let's Introduce Ourselves

Student Name(s):

These are five things we want the class we are going to communicate with to know about our class:

1.

2.

3.

4.

We think these are important to tell the other class because:

We would like to know these things about the class with whom we are going to be communicating:

1.

2.

3.

4.

5.

A message we might send with information about our class and with questions about the other class is:

Activity Sheet

Questions About the Middle Ages

Student Name(s):

These are the three questions that we want to ask the other class about the Middle Ages:

1.

2.

3.

We think these are good questions to ask the other class because:

The message we are going to send the class with these questions is:

Activity Sheet

Thanks for Working with Us Template

Dear _____:

Thanks for working with us to learn about the Middle Ages.

We thought the best part of learning this way was_____

Our favorite fact that we learned about the Middle Ages is_____

_____

If you find out more information about the Middle Ages or would like to ask us some other questions, let us know.

Sincerely,

(Names of students)

WHERE DO I FIND OUT MORE ABOUT E-MAIL?

Here is a list of resources mentioned in this unit, along with other materials on how e-mail works and how you can integrate it into the classroom.

A+ Locator

www.vrd.org/locator/index.html

Find an expert and send an e-mail.

Ask an Expert

www.askanexpert.com/

Browse through the categories to find experts in a variety of fields.

ePALS

www.epals.com/

Search the database to find a classroom with which your students can communicate.

Everything E-Mail

http://everythingemail.net/

This is just what you need to know to get started and use e-mail.

Ideas for Collaborative E-mail and WWW Language Learning

www.techlearning.com/db_area/archives/WCE/verity_archives/davies.htm

An article that discusses different models for e-mail use in the classroom.

Learn the Net—Harness E-Mail

www.learnthenet.com/english/index.html

When you select the "Harness E-Mail" link, you'll access lots of step-by-step guides to using e-mail successfully.

Liszt

www.listz.com/

Find a mailing list on almost any topic imaginable.

Tile.net

http://tile.net/

Search for mailing lists.

webTeacher—Electronic Mail

www.webteacher.org/winnet/indextc.html

Select the link labeled "Electronic Mail" to find out how to use e-mail.

BASIC E-MAIL GLOSSARY

Address

Where an e-mail message will be sent. In order to send an e-mail message, you need to have the address of the recipient, just like you need to have the street address of the person you want to send a letter to via postal mail.

Address Book

A storage space in an e-mail program that allows you to store the names and e-mail addresses of those you e-mail regularly.

Attachment

A file sent from your computer to the computer of the person receiving the e-mail message. When you send an attachment, the recipient can open a file you created— a word processing document, an image, a database, a spreadsheet, and so on.

CC: (Carbon Copy)

Just like sending a business memo and adding a CC: to the recipient list. The message will also be sent to the address that you put in the CC: line of an e-mail message template.

Emoticon (Emotion Icon)

Using computer characters to display an emotion or reaction, for example, :-] . Turn it sideways and see a happy face.

Filter

Criteria you develop so the e-mail program places messages in specific folders. Usually the criteria are related to the author or the subject of a message.

Folder

A place to store and organize e-mail messages. E-mail folders work the same way as folders in a file cabinet. In the e-mail program you create folders on specific themes or topics. Then you store messages in appropriate folders instead of keeping them all in your Inbox.

Forward

Passing a message that you have received on to someone else. (Remember, before you forward a message, you should ask the original author if it is acceptable to do so.)

From

In an e-mail template, the field for the e-mail address, and sometimes the name, of the person sending the message.

Inbox

Where e-mail messages are stored when they are downloaded from the mail server to your computer.

Listserv (see Mailing List)

Mailing List

A free subscription service that connects people with a common interest through e-mail. After subscribing, members of the mailing list send and receive messages from other subscribers to the list.

Message

The note, letter, or other information that is sent from the sender to the recipient via e-mail.

Outbox

Where messages that have been sent are stored.

Reply

A response to an e-mail message.

Reply to All

A type of response to an e-mail message. When an e-mail message is sent to a group of people, you can respond by sending the message to everyone in the "to" field or just to the person who wrote the original message. If you respond to everyone on the "to" field, then you are replying to all.

Send

The command to deliver an e-mail message.

Subject

The field in an e-mail message template for information regarding the topic of the message. Being specific in the subject line helps the recipient know something about the message before he reads it.

To

The field in an e-mail message template for the e-mail address, and sometimes name, of the person(s) to whom the message is being sent.

Unit 4

Looking into Chat and Instant Messaging

Oh my gosh, the students you know want to use chat and instant messaging. You're nervous about it because all you hear is how only bad things happen when students take part in this type of virtual communication. What you haven't heard about are the interesting and educational opportunities that can (and do) happen with chat and instant messaging. This unit takes a look at what chat and instant messaging are, why kids like to use them, and how to incorporate them into your classroom, library, or home.

WHAT IS CHAT?

So, what exactly is chat? Chat allows you to talk with others on the Internet in what is called "real time." That means you are chatting with them live—everyone in on the chat is on the Internet having a conversation at the same time. It's like a conference call, except instead of speaking over the phone, you are typing messages (or speaking out loud) to communicate over the Internet.

People have set up special chat sites to talk with others who have like interests–whether it is teaching math and science or raising a poodle. There are chat sites for children and chat sites for adults. When thinking about joining in a chat discussion, some things to consider include:

- Who is the sponsor of the chat? Consider if the sponsor is a well-known organization that has experience working with teachers or students on the topic of the chat. If the sponsor is a business or individual, consider how well they will be able to manage the discussion and what their purpose is in providing the chat space to children and/or adults.

- Is there someone "moderating" the chat to make sure that the discussion stays on target? Even in face-to-face conversations it's easy to go off on tangents and forget what the theme of the discussion is supposed to be. In chat, this happens readily and it's useful to have someone in charge who can get the chatters back to the topic they are supposed to be considering.
- Do you need a special kind of software in order to take part in the chat? Some chat sites require downloading software in order to take full advantage of special features such as voice and images. If this is necessary, consider if you are going to be able to use these special features before deciding to take part in the chat.

There are actually different types of chat that children, or adults, take part in:

- Text chat (words on the screen)
- Graphical chat (each person in the chat room has an icon that represents him)
- Audio/video chat (where the chatters are heard and/or seen by each other)

No matter which chat format you are using, some aspects almost always work the same way. For example, after you decide to take part in a chat, a window opens up on the computer screen and asks for login information. This is used to identify the chatter to the rest of the participants.

Fig. 4.1
Rules For Chat And Instant Messaging Safety

Remember not to give out your home address or phone number.

The name and address of your school should not be included in a chat or instant messaging conversation.

Only give out your e-mail address to people you know.

Use nicknames when talking to strangers.

Talk to adults about the conversations that you have while chatting online.

Talk to an adult if something that happened while chatting bothers you.

When you are working with students to teach them how to use chat effectively and safely point out that they shouldn't use their real name when they log onto a chat site. Since there is no way to know who is sitting at other computers, it's important to not give out any personal information when taking part in a chat.

WHAT IS INSTANT MESSAGING?

The next question you might be asking yourself is, "if that's chat, what's instant messaging?" Here's the answer: Instant messaging (also known as IM) is a form of chat where users decide with whom they want to chat and they can see who is online when they are.

To use instant messaging:

- You need to install a piece of software—often ICQ (pronounced I-seek-you) or AOL Instant Messenger (AIM)—on the computer. This software, which is free, is available for download from ICQ or AOL.
- After the software is installed, the user (you or your students) invites friends, family, other students from around the world, and so forth, to be on a "buddy list." (In order to be added to a "buddy list" the person being invited to join the list has to have the software installed on her computer.)
- After adding names to the "buddy list," whenever the child is online she can tell who on her "buddy list" is also online. When two or more people on the list are online at the same time, a chat can be initiated.

Instant messaging software provides great opportunities to start chat sessions in a safe environment. By being able to chat only with those who have been invited to join a "buddy list," a child can be sure that who he is talking to is someone with whom he has an established relationship. If you are working in a school, you might create a "buddy list" for a school (or many schools) in another state or country. Then, when you both (or all) are online, you initiate a chat between the students in the two, three, four, or more classrooms.

WHAT CAN I DO WITH CHAT AND INSTANT MESSAGING?

Now that you know a little bit about chat and instant messaging, you still might be asking why is it a good idea for kids to use these tools? The best way to answer that question is to investigate some of the chat opportunities that are available to children.

One Internet resource that has a strong chat component is the **Read In**. The **Read In** is an annual event that brings students and authors together to talk about books and reading. Students around the world participate by accessing the **Read In** chat site where they talk in real time with participating authors.

Another site that provides great chatting opportunities for children is **NASA Quest**. Teachers, students, and parents are invited to register (it's free) to take part in chats with NASA employees about their work. Students have chatted with engineers, pilots, astronauts, and researchers.

By incorporating chat into their educational framework, these two sites provide kids with the chance to communicate with professionals with whom they might not otherwise have a chance to talk. Inviting authors of the caliber of those connected to the **Read In** to a school or library is an expensive proposition. NASA employees aren't commonly available to speak to classrooms. Combine that with the fact that students not only get to talk with professionals to find out what their lives and work are like, but they also get to communicate with other students from around the world who are taking part in the same chat sessions. This creates a powerful communications event.

Even a site like **FreeZone,** which provides access to monitored chat rooms specifically for children, has educational value. There are FreeZone rooms where children can go to chat about what's on their mind. There are also scheduled chat sessions on topics from martial arts to homeschooling. In this and other text-based chats, children write out their thoughts and ideas and read what others have to say. This gives them a chance to practice the fundamental language arts skills of reading and writing.

Some might say that one of the problems related to chat is that students tend to misspell words and use a new form of shorthand to communicate their thoughts and ideas. This is true. Because chat communication moves at a rapid pace, it requires using a kind of shorthand. Misspellings are also likely to occur. The way children, and adults, communicate via chat is something that needs to be addressed with students. Students need to realize that chat is a method of communication that is not appropriate for all situations. By incorporating chat into the classroom and the daily lives of children, opportunities are created for teaching children about different methods of communication and when each is appropriate to use.

Another way to begin an exploration of communication techniques is by using chat transcripts, available on the Web, as a tool for discussing communication, writing styles, grammar, and language. A search for transcripts at **Yahooligans!** leads to a list of chat sessions that have been held with celebrities in various fields, from John Glenn to the Backstreet Boys and from Cathy Rigby to Judy Blume.

Give students a chance to read through transcripts of chat conversations and facilitate discussions about the differences between chat and the same conversation over the phone, in person, through letters, or by e-mail. Ask students to replicate the conversation in one of these other forms to see clearly what the differences are. Chat transcripts can also be used in lessons related to story dialog. Students can use a chat transcript as a story starter. They would then incorporate parts of the transcript as dialog within the story.

IM software automatically saves transcripts of instant messaging sessions. After students take part in an instant messaging session, print the transcript for students to find spelling and grammar errors. The purpose of this lesson would not be to teach students about improving spelling and grammar during a chat session; instead, it would center on the idea that in some forms of communication it's important to make sure that spelling and grammar are accurately handled and in other forms of communication it is not.

The following lesson plan is an example of how to integrate chat into the classroom.

LESSON PLAN—USING CHAT TO LEARN ABOUT A TOPIC

Overview

Students participate in a **NASA Quest** chat to learn what it's like to work at NASA. They also study a chat transcript to discuss how communicating via chat is different from other forms of communication.

Before Getting Started

Visit the **NASA Quest Chat Center**, *http://quest.arc.nasa.gov/qchats/*, to find out what chats are scheduled to take place over the next few weeks or months. Select a chat that you think is appropriate for your students. Register for the chat session. Read through the page on how to prepare for a **NASA Quest** chat. This provides you with the information you need in order to effectively prepare for the chat event. As you prepare make sure to consider who is going to be typing in the questions and information that students contribute to the chat session. Will you be doing all the typing or will students do some of this themselves? Students will have to be prepared for how this is going to be handled.

Student Prerequisites

- Beginning knowledge of aviation history
- Beginning knowledge of space exploration history and careers

---

Lesson Sidebar 10 The Critical Thinking Connection—Chat

For many students chat is an entertainment activity. They don't often think about the issues that plague many adults when they think of (or use) chat. Integrating chat into the classroom gives you a chance to help students understand how to chat safely and intelligently. Use any lessons that include a chat component to point out to students how easy it is for anyone to log into a chat room and present a personality that isn't really her own. Teach students to think critically about whom they are talking with and how they can be certain that the person is who she says she is. Also, use the chat lesson to help students understand different forms of communication and when one form is more appropriate than another. Make sure that they have the skills to determine when grammar and language styles are appropriate and when they are not appropriate.

Technology Requirements

- Individual or small group computer access
- Internet access
- Access to the World Wide Web

Activity Sheets

- *What's the Difference*
- *Questions for NASA*
- *We Didn't Know That Before*

Grade Level

- Grades 4 and 5

Curriculum Connections

- Language Arts
- Science
- History/Social Science

Internet Skills

- Navigation
- Chat

Critical Thinking Skills

- Information analysis
- Research

Student Outcomes

- Ability to articulate orally and in writing the differences among varieties of communication.
- Familiarity with the features and uses of chat.
- Understanding how to pose a question in order to elicit an appropriate and useful response.
- Knowledge of aviation history.
- Knowledge of space exploration science and careers.

Extension Activities

- Students read a chat transcript available on the **NASA Quest** site and create a biography of one of the employees who took part in the chat session.
- After reading a chat transcript, students use pieces of the chat conversation and turn it into dialog for a story or the basis of a play on space exploration.
- Students research the history of space exploration and/or NASA and create written or oral reports on the topic.

Activity Procedure

1. Explain to students that in a few days they will be taking part in a live chat with an employee of NASA and that there are certain things they need to do to get ready. Facilitate a discussion on a definition of chat. Ask students if they have ever taken part in a chat or instant messaging event. Have students who have been involved in either describe their experiences to the rest of the class. Ask them to discuss what they like and don't like about chat and instant messaging.

2. Show students the transcript from the **NASA Quest** chat on December 9, 1999, with Orville and Wilbur Wright, *http:// quest.arc.nasa.gov/aero/chats/12–16–99wb.html*. Explain the different sections of the chat transcript and point out how to tell who is "speaking" during a chat session.

3. Ask students to take turns reading the transcript aloud.

4. After the reading is completed, distribute the *What's the Difference?* activity sheet. Divide the class into groups and have each group use the worksheet to record the ways they think chat conversation is different than face-to-face, e-mail, phone, and letter communication.

5. Bring the class back together to discuss the lists they developed. Be sure to point out that chat conversations usually happen quickly and that means students have to think and type quickly. As a result, sentences might not always be written as clearly as they would be if the conversation were taking place in a different medium.

6. Show the class the biographical information available on the NASA employee with whom they will be chatting. Have students read the information.

7. Distribute the activity sheet *Questions for NASA*. Send the class back into groups and ask each group to come up with as many questions as possible that they would like to ask the person with whom they will be chatting.

Chat Notes for Teachers

- This lesson is perfect for a one-computer classroom with a computer projection system available. Students can prepare for the chat session online and then take part in the session as a full class, viewing the chat on a screen in the classroom.
- If students are sitting separately at computers, you will want to make sure that they don't add to the chat unless appropriate and at the proper time.
- At the third-grade level focus on chat transcripts with students. Use AOL Instant Messaging or ICQ to connect with another classroom in your community or in another part of the country. After your students have had a chat with another class using IM software, print out the transcript of the chat and talk about the process and the product.

---

8. Bring the class back together and have each group read the questions they developed. Have the class pick one question from each group to ask when chatting at **NASA Quest**. Have students write down the one question that their group will ask from the *Questions for NASA* activity sheet.

9. On the day of the chat explain to students how you will be handling the typing of the questions.

10. Take part in the chat.

11. After the chat is over, distribute another copy of the *What's the Difference?* activity sheet to each group. Have the groups fill out the activity sheet again to see if they have new ideas about differences between chat and other forms of communication.

12. Bring the class back together and facilitate a discussion about the students' chat experience and their new ideas about the differences between chat and other forms of communication.

13. Distribute the *We Didn't Know That Before* activity sheet. Send the class back into their groups and ask each group to record information about what they learned during the chat and what they thought of the chat experience.

14. Bring the class back together to talk about the information they recorded on the worksheet.

Website Alternatives

The following Websites listed may be substituted for **NASA Quest** to integrate chat into the classroom.

AfriCam AfriSchool (History/Social Science, Language Arts, Science)

www.africam.com/mirror/afrischool/index.html

Join **AfriSchool** (it's free) and your class will be assigned a volunteer wildlife expert who will meet in a chat room with your students on a regular basis. The **AfriSchool** chat room is a good place to get students started on their use of chat. Since your class will be the only ones chatting with the wildlife expert, students will have an opportunity to get used to the chat format in a controlled environment.

Chat with Jack Hanna Transcript (Language Arts, Science)

www.seaworld.org/Chats/jackhannachat.html

Before reading this chat transcript with students, engage the class in a KWL (Know, Want to Know, Learned) exercise. Ask students to tell you what they know about sea animals. Then have students brainstorm what they want to learn about sea animals. After reading the chat transcript, ask students to discuss what they learned. Did they learn anything that was on their "want to know" list? Facilitate a discussion about the kinds of information that are generated in a chat and that can be retrieved by reading a chat transcript.

Koko's Earth Day Chat Transcript (Language Arts, Science)

www.koko.org/news/aol.html

In 1998 Koko, the gorilla, took part in a chat in honor of Earth Day. Use this transcript to talk with students about communication between people and animals as well as communication using chat. Discuss how Koko took part in the chat and if that participation can be considered a valid form of communication.

Read In (Language Arts)

www.readin.org/

The culmination of the **Read In** is the annual day of author chats. However, other chats are hosted during the year. You can take part in these chats so that both you and your students feel comfortable with the format before the official **Read In** day.

Activity Sheet

What's the Difference?

Student Name(s):

Think about each of the different types of communication listed in the chart below. Consider what it's like to use each communication technique. Then write in the chart all the things you can think of about communicating each way. For example, for chat you might write, "Have to type fast." For face-to-face you might write, "Get to see the faces a person makes while talking."

Chat	Phone	E-mail	Letter	Face-to-Face

Record what you think is the number-one biggest difference between:

Chat & Phone	Chat & E-mail	Chat & Letter	Chat & Face-to-Face

Use the space below to tell what your favorite form of communication is and why.

Activity Sheet

Questions for NASA

Student Name(s):

We are going to be chatting with_____.

During our chat we think we will find information about:

During our chat we would like to get the answers to these questions:

1.

2.

3.

4.

5.

We think these are good questions to ask because:

The one question from our list that we are most interested in finding the answer to is:

Activity Sheet

We Didn't Know That Before

Student Name(s):

We chatted with _____

The most interesting part of the chat was:

This is something we learned during the chat that we didn't know before:

We think chatting is a good/bad way to learn about something because:

If we had the chance to use chat in our class again, we would want to because:

WHERE DO I FIND OUT MORE ABOUT CHAT AND INSTANT MESSAGING?

Here is a list of resources mentioned in this unit, materials on how e-mail and instant messaging work, and ways you can integrate these tools into the classroom.

AOL Instant Messenger

www.aol.com/aim/home.html

Even if you don't use AOL you can download this software for instant messaging.

The Beginner's Guide to Chat

http://coverage.cnet.com/Content/Reports/Guides/BegChat/?tag=st.int.3781.txt.begchat

Learn the basics and more in this overview of chat and how it works.

FreeZone

www.freezone.com/

FreeZone sponsors moderated chats for children.

ICQ

www.icq.com/

Use ICQ to send and receive instant messages.

The Read In

www.readin.org/

Sign up for the **Read In** and take part in chat sessions with a variety of popular children's book authors.

NASA Quest

http://quest.arc.nasa.gov/

Join in on chats with NASA employees in lots of different fields of work.

WebTeacher—Internet Chat Groups

www.Webteacher.org/winnet/indextc.html

Scroll down the page to choose the "Internet Chat Groups" link from the right hand column. The link leads to a resource that shows you how easy it is to set up your own chat room.

Yahooligans! Chat

http://search.yahooligans.com/search/ligans?p=chat

A search for chat on **Yahooligans!** generates a list of chat transcripts and sites that provide chat for children.

BASIC CHAT GLOSSARY

AOL Instant Messenger (AIM)

AOL's instant messaging software. You do not have to be an AOL subscriber to use the software.

Buddy List

After installing instant messaging software, you can create a list of friends, family members, classrooms, etc. to communicate with using the instant messaging software. You can set up the software so that only people on your Buddy List can send you instant messages.

Chat

Talking with other people over the Internet in "real time."

ICQ

A popular piece of instant messaging software.

Instant Messaging (IM)

Sending messages in "real" time to others who are on the Internet at the same time.

Appendix A

Lesson Plans, Curriculum Integration, and Citation Resources

Abilock, Debbie. (2000a) *NoodleBib* [Online]. Available: *www. noodletools.com/noodlebib/index.html* [2000, August 2]

_____. (2000b) *Library Goal Research* [Online]. Available: *http:// nuevaschool.org/~debbie/library/research/research.html* [2000, August 2]

American Fidelity Education Services. (2000) *Education World* [Online]. Available: *www.education-world.com/* [2000, August 2]

Classroom Connect. (1999) *Citing Internet Resources* [Online]. Available: *www.connectedteacher.com/newsletter/citeintres.asp* [2000, August 2]

Dias, Laura B. (1999) "Integrating Technology: Some Things You Should Know." *Learning & Leading with Technology* (November): 10–13.

Dodge, Bernie. (2000) *The Web Quest Page* [Online]. Available: *http:/ /edweb.sdsu.edu/webquest/webquest.html* [2000, August 2]

Felt, Elizabeth Caulfield and Sarah C. Symans. "Teaching Students to Use the Internet as a Research Tool" *Learning & Leading with Technology*. (March): 10–13.

Francek, Mark. (2000) "The Web as an Instructional Tool" *Learning & Leading with Technology*. (March): 6–9.

Harris, Judi. (2000a) "Taboo Topic No Longer: Why Telecollaborative Projects Sometimes Fail." *Learning & Leading with Technology* (February): 58–61.

_____. (2000b) *Virtual Architecture's Web Home* [Online]. Available: *http://ccwf.cc.utexas.edu/~jbharris/Virtual-Architecture/index.html* [2000, August 2]

International Society for Technology in Education. (2000) *National Educational Technology Standards for Students: Connecting Curriculum and Technology.* Eugene, Oreg.: ISTE.

Internet Public Library. (2000) *Citing Electronic Resources* [Online]. Available: *www.ipl.org/ref/QUE/FARQ/netciteFARQ.html* [2000, August 2]

Li, Xia and Nancy Crane. (1996) *Electronic Styles: A Handbook for Citing Electronic Information.* Medford, N.J.: Information Today, Inc.

Miller, Elizabeth. *Thematic Units for Primary Grades.* (1999) [Online]. Available: *www.libsci.sc.edu/miller/Unitlink.htm* [2000, August 2]

McRel. (2000) *Connections+* [Online]. Available: *www.mcrel.org/resources/plus/index.asp?option=404* [2000, August 2]

Odasz, Frank. (1999/2000) "Collaborative Internet Tools." *Learning & Leading with Technology* (December-January): 10–17.

Pacific Bell. (2000) Blue Web'N. [Online]. Available: *www.kn.pacbell.com/wired/bluewebn/.* [2000, August 2]

Roblyer, M. D. (1999) *Integrating Technology Across the Curriculum: A Database of Strategies and Lesson Plans* [CD-ROM]. Prentice Hall.

Rogers, Claire. (2000) "Educators Find the Internet a Valuable Education Tool." *Educators Guide to Computers in the Classroom* (September): 8–10.

Schubert, Nancy. (2000) *Nick Nacks: Telecollaborate* [Online]. Available: *http://home.talkcity.com/academydr/nicknacks/NNindex.html* [2000, August 2]

S.C.O.R.E. (2000) *CyberGuides: Teacher Guides and Student Activities* [Online]. Available: *www.sdcoe.k12.ca.us/score/cyberguide.html* [2000, August 2]

U.S. Department of Education. (2000) *The Gateway to Educational Materials* [Online]. Available: *www.thegateway.org/* [2000, August 2]

Appendix B

Information Literacy Resources

American Association of School Librarians. (1999) *Information Literacy Standards for Student Learning*. Chicago: American Library Association.

Bowens, Elva Marie. (2000) "Research, Analysis, Communication: Meeting Standards with Technology." *Learning & Leading with Technology* (May): 6–9.

Breivik, Patricia Senn. (2000) *National Forum on Information Literacy* [Online]. Available: *www.infolit.org/* [2000, December 12]

California Technology Assistance Project. (2000) *Information Literacy* [Online]. Available: *http://ctap.fcoe.k12.ca.us/ctap/Info.Lit/infolit.html* [2000, August 2]

College of Education, University of Oregon. (N/A) *Information Literacy* [Online]. Available: *http://interact.uoregon.edu/MediaLit/FA/MLInfolit.html* [2000, August 2]

Eisenberg, Michael B. and Robert E. Berkowitz. (2000a) *The Big6 Collection: The Best of the Big6 Newsletter*. Worthington, Ohio: Linworth Publishing Co.

_____. (2000b) *The Big6 Skills Information Problem Solving Approach* [Online]. Available: *www.big6.com/* [2000, August 2]

_____. (1999) *The New Improved Big6 Workshop Handbook*. Worthington, Ohio: Linworth Publishing Co.

Eisenberg, Michael B. and Doug Johnson. (1996) *Computer Skills for Information Problem-Solving: Learning and Teaching Technology in Context* [Online]. ERIC Digest. Available: *www.ed.gov/databases/ERIC_Digests/ed392463.html* [2000, December 12]

Eisenberg, Michael B., Robert E. Berkowitz, and Barbara A. Jansen (1999) *Teaching Information & Technology Skills: The Big6 in Elementary School*. Worthington, Ohio: Linworth Publishing Co.

Georgia Department of Education. (1999) *Information Literacy Skills Index* [Online]. Available: *www.glc.k12.ga.us/qstd-int/ancill/ils/ind-ils.htm* [2000, August 2]

Gibson, Melissa R. (2000) *Research Buddy* [Online]. Available: *www.squires.fayette.k12.ky.us/library/research/research.htm* [2000, August 2]

Hancock, Vicki E. (1993) *Information Literacy for Lifelong Learning* [Online]. ERIC Digest. Available: *www.ed.gov/databases/ERIC_Digests/ed358870.html* [2000, August 2]

Heller, Norma. (1998) *Technology Connections for Grades 3–5 : Research Projects and Activities*. Englewood, Colo.: Libraries Unlimited.

Johnson, Doug. (2000) *Mankato Schools Information Literacy Curriculum Guidelines* [Online]. Available: *www.isd77.k12.mn.us/resources/infocurr/infolit.html* [2000, August 2]

———. (1999) "A Curriculum Built Not to Last." *School Library Journal* (April): 26–30.

Langhorne, Mary Jo, ed. (1998) *Developing an Information Literacy Program K–12 : A How-To-Do-It Manual and CD-Rom Package*. New York: Neal-Schuman.

McGregor, Joy. (1999) "Teaching the Research Process: Helping Students Become Lifelong Learners." *NASSP Bulletin* (March): 27–35.

O'Sullivan, Michael and Thomas Scott. (2000) *Teaching Information Literacy: A Critical Evaluation* [Online]. Multimedia Schools. Available: *www.infotoday.com/MMSchools/mar00/osullivan&scott.htm* [2000, August 2]

Roth, Lorie. (1999) "Educating the Cut-and-Paste Generation." *Library Journal* (November 1): 42.

Small, Ruth V. and Marilyn P. Arnone. (2000) *Turning Kids on to Research: The Power of Motivation*. Englewood, Colo.: Libraries Unlimited.

Smith, Drew, ed. (2000) *Directory of Online Resources for Information Literacy* [Online]. Available: *www.cas.usf.edu/lis/il/* [2000, August 2]

Thompson, Helen M. and Susan A. Henley. (2000) *Fostering Information Literacy: Connecting National Standards, Goals 2000, and the SCANS Report*. Englewood, Colo: Libraries Unlimited.

Office of the Superintendent of Public Instruction, Olympia, Wash. and the Washington Library Media Association. (1996) *Essential Skills for Information Literacy* [Online]. Available: *www.wlma.org/literacy/eslintro.htm* [2000, August 2]

Subject Index

Website Index

About the Author

Linda W. Braun is an educational technology consultant with LEO: Librarians & Educators Online. She works with schools and libraries to provide consulting, training, and project management on a variety of topics from curriculum design to basic searching techniques, educational Web site design, and the future of library services. Along with her work for LEO, Linda currently teaches in the Lesley University, Graduate School of Education, Technology in Education program and for the University of Maine in their Library and Information Technology distance education program. Before working for LEO, Linda worked in public libraries in New York, Massachusetts, and New Jersey.